Costumes of Everyday Life
An Illustrated History of Working Clothes

By the same author:

COSTUME: AN ILLUSTRATED SURVEY FROM ANCIENT TIMES TO THE TWENTIETH CENTURY

Costumes of Everyday Life

An Illustrated History of Working Clothes

Margot Lister

Publishers   **PLAYS, INC.**   *Boston*

First American edition published by
PLAYS, INC. 1972
Second impression November 1972

Printed in Great Britain by Butler & Tanner Ltd., Frome and London

Library of Congress Catalog Card Number: 77-172485
ISBN: 0-8238-0097-0

CONTENTS

INTRODUCTION

This book is a companion to my *Costume: An Illustrated Survey from Ancient Times to the Twentieth Century*. It traces the development of the dress of functionaries, with emphasis on that worn by artisans, labourers, minor officials, tradesmen, citizens in urban employment, indoor and outdoor servants, although some examples from the professions are shown. They are shown in clothes suitable to their way of life from the Middle Ages to the early years of the twentieth century. A brief mention of some of the chief trends and events in this wide span of years is made here, and some information about social changes, customs and conditions given in the introduction to chapters.

The drawings have individual descriptive captions, and illustrate for the most part the dress of England and France, but some examples are of German, Italian, French, Dutch, Flemish or Spanish origin or have items in them that passed from one country to another. Some Irish, Welsh and Scottish dress is shown and, in the latter part of the book, some American costume. Specific national dress has not been included, as this is a matter for separate study.

Included in the dress worn from feudal times to the mid-seventeenth century is that of the gentlepeople who served in great houses as chamberlains, marshals of the household, chief stewards, financial comptrollers, legal advisers and others in responsible attendance on their lord. Under feudalism they were the forerunners of today's financial advisers, estate bailiffs, higher civil servants, scholars and legal experts.

A point has been made in the illustrations of finding examples of costumes adapted to an active mode of life, such as shorter and more manageable dresses for women than those in current fashion. A number of these have been illustrated, though there seem to have been many people who were satisfied with a partial adaptation or none at all.

A certain mingling of styles can be seen among the poorer classes, whose clothes were often handed down to them by wealthier people or kept as family possessions and worn for more than one generation.

The book covers the emergence of Western Europe from the six centuries of chaos that followed the fall of Rome, the long slow climb to the Renaissance, the development of nationalism and finally of imperialism. In these centuries, commerce among nations prospered and wavered; boundaries were made, altered and made again; wars of conquest and of religion occupied the kings and the Papacy, whose ambition was to re-create the Roman Empire. But with the discovery of the New World across the Atlantic and of other distant lands the dream of reviving Roman sovereignty in Europe was abandoned, and the nations began to compete with each other in founding empires across the seas.

In due course, the successes and failures of colonisation, the trading interests with new countries, and all the opportunities and risks for the individual that they involved were to have a profound effect on the habits and lives of ordinary people.

It is hoped that the book will be useful to artists, costume-designers, directors of costume plays and pageants, sociologists and history students.

I am most grateful for the help derived from the many interesting works of reference and description that have been available to me, also for the facilities given in museums and libraries.

GLOSSARY

Aiguillettes: bobbin-shaped fastenings for open sleeves or fronts of dresses, sixteenth century.

Bag-sleeves: bag-shaped sleeves with bands at wrists, sometimes with seam open, mid-fourteenth–fifteenth centuries.

Baldrick: belt worn in decorative form from right shoulder to opposite hip, fifteenth century. Later used as ammunition-belt.

Barbette: linen band passing under the chin and fastened on the top of the head, worn by women, twelfth–fourteenth centuries.

Bases: full circular kilts of padded segments worn by men, early sixteenth century.

Bertha: deep circular collar worn by women, usually below shoulders, seventeenth, mid-nineteenth, early twentieth centuries.

Bliaut: twelfth century body-fitting dress with pleated skirts worn by both sexes.

Bolero: short open jacket worn open and ending above or at the waist.

Bongrâce headdress: flat square headdress with veil at back, worn by women, late fifteenth–early seventeenth centuries.

Bonnet-shaped cap: head-fitting cap with frills framing face, eighteenth century.

Braccae, Braes: loose trousers ending at ankles, early times to thirteenth century.

Brandenburg: loose-fitting greatcoat, late seventeenth century.

Bucket-top boots: boots with wide tops, mid-seventeenth century.

Bustle: framework worn beneath a draped skirt to form a protuberance at the back, late nineteenth century.

Butterfly spur-leathers: large butterfly-shaped pieces of leather worn over front of instep and holding spurs at the back.

Byecocket: hat with long peak in front, upturned brim at back and long cone-shaped crown, fifteenth century.

Canions: close-fitting upper leg-coverings worn over complete hose, late sixteenth century.

Canons: garters with wide lace frill hanging downward, worn below knees and looking like frills to the breeches.

Cassock: name given to plain gown, fifteenth century, and loose outer wrap, sixteenth–seventeenth centuries.

Caul: women's jewelled net head-covering, fourteenth–fifteenth centuries; small round ornamented cap worn at back of head by women, sixteenth and seventeenth centuries.

Chaperon: hat contrived from winding long 'liripipe' (q.v.) round cap, later made as complete hat, mid-fourteenth–fifteenth centuries.

Chemisette: insert of linen, lawn, lace, gauze or other delicate material to fill in neck and front of bodice, nineteenth–twentieth centuries.

Chignon: knot or coil of hair pinned up on the head.

Circular cloak: cloak with aperture for the head or cloak made of segments of a circle. Early times to fourteenth century.

Cloak-bag breeches: full breeches banded at the knee, usually bordered with rosettes or bows ending in 'points' (q.v.).

Coif: close-fitting cap of white linen, later embroidered or made in black silk, thirteenth–seventeenth centuries.

Copotain: tall-crowned hat with moderate-sized, often flexible brim, later sixteenth–early seventeenth centuries.

Cornet: small version of fontange (q.v.), late seventeenth century.

Cotehardie: body-fitting gown for men or women, fourteenth-fifteenth centuries.

Crinoline: petticoat stiffened by bands of cane, steel or whalebone, 1850s–1860s.

Cyclas: outer gown, usually sleeveless, with side or front openings, thirteenth-fourteenth centuries.

Dagged edges, dagges: edges of material cut in points, scallops or castellated shapes.

Dalmatic: late Roman and Byzantine gown, later a church vestment. Gowns resembling it worn from tenth to thirteenth centuries.

Dolman: woman's cape, late nineteenth, early twentieth centuries.

Dolman sleeves: sleeves cut in one with a garment with deep arm-hole.

Dormeuse cap: women's deep-crowned cap set back on head, late eighteenth century.

Doublet: man's garment, usually padded, ending at waist or hips, late fifteenth–early seventeenth centuries.

Dutch breeches: loose breeches not caught in at the knees, early seventeenth century.

Escoffion: small, cylindrical cap, worn by women, 1550s–1570s.

Falling band: ruff or collar lying flat or turned down.

Farthingale: petticoat stiffened with bands of steel or cane, from early sixteenth century to early seventeenth; could be in form of 'bolster' tied on at waist.

7

From late sixteenth century could be in 'wheel' shape or in form of roll tied on at waist.

Flat cap: beret-shaped cap with very narrow brim.

Fontange: head-fitting muslin, silk or lace cap with tall front decoration.

French hood: headdress with curved stiffened front and veil or cap at the back, late fifteenth, greater part of sixteenth centuries.

Frock: name given to eighteenth century men's coat with flat round collar and skirts moderately flared.

Gable headdress: headdress with stiffened pyramidal front, worn by women, late fifteenth, early sixteenth centuries.

Galloon: edging of gold, silver or colour.

Ganache: loose outer garment with sleeves contrived from side-seams, thirteenth–fourteenth centuries.

Gilet: inner waistcoat, nineteenth century.

Goblet cuffs: cuffs extending over the hands in goblet-shape from tight-fitting sleeves, fourteenth–fifteenth and early nineteenth centuries.

Golilla: lace collar with square-cut base, early seventeenth century.

Gorget: linen neck-covering coming up over ears and pinned to hair or at top of head, thirteenth–fifteenth centuries.

Hanging sleeves: sleeves of over-gown left hanging or put on over other sleeves.

Head-rail: Saxon head-veil for women.

Hennin: cone-shaped or cylindrical headdress for women, fifteenth century.

Hérigault: loose outer garment with cape sleeves, thirteenth century.

Houppeland: voluminous gown worn by men and women, late fourteenth century, greater part of fifteenth century.

Jerkin: outer garment, usually sleeveless, covering doublet, sixteenth–seventeenth centuries. When sleeved could be worn without doublet.

Jump jacket: short, close-fitting jacket resembling a sleeved waistcoat, worn from late seventeenth century.

Kirtle: petticoat or under-skirt, sixteenth–seventeenth centuries.

Lappet: appendage of cap, at side or back.

Liripipe: long 'tail' depending from hood or *chaperon*, fourteenth–fifteenth centuries.

Mahoytered sleeves: sleeves puffed at the shoulders, latter part of fifteenth and mid-sixteenth centuries.

Marie Stuart cap: cap fitting the head with downward curve or point in centre of forehead, mid-sixteenth, early seventeenth centuries.

Melon hose: see 'Round-hose', 'Trunk-hose'.

Mule: slipper with upper in front only and raised or flat heel.

Nebulae headdress: narrow halo-shaped headdress of gauze, fourteenth century.

Nether-stocks: stockings joined by points to upper-stocks (q.v.).

Paning, Panes, Pane: material showing through 'slashings' in garments.

Partlet: guimpe or insert of lawn, linen or gauze to fill in the top of the bodice in front, late fifteenth–early seventeenth centuries.

Pattens: separate platform-soles put on over shoes to raise the feet from the ground.

Peascod belly: padded, downward point protruding over doublet-belt, late sixteenth century.

Penner: case of metal and leather worn at the belt to hold quill pens.

Petticoat breeches: loose breeches cut to resemble a kilt, mid-seventeenth century.

Phrygian cap: cap with coxcomb peak in front. Persia, Greece, early European dress, French Revolution.

Pinner: flat cap of lawn, lace or embroidery, worn on the top of the head, first half of eighteenth century.

Points: device of laces and eyelet-holes to fasten sleeves to shoulders, tights to under-doublet, etc.

Polonaise: over-dress with back pleats and drapery, eighteenth and late nineteenth centuries.

Pomander: orange stuck with cloves to dispel odours; perforated sphere of goldsmith's work, containing scented substances.

Pompon: small hair-ornament of lace, flowers and ribbons, greater part of eighteenth century.

Poulaines: very long-toed shoes, fifteenth century.

Pourpoint: under-doublet, fifteenth–sixteenth centuries.

Ramshorn headdress: cap with coiled earpieces, thirteenth century.

Redingote: outer coat, late eighteenth–nineteenth centuries.

Rhinegrave breeches: see 'Petticoat breeches'.

Rondel: crescent-shaped, circular or halo-shaped headdress, fourteenth–fifteenth centuries.

Round-eared cap: head-fitting cap, first half of eighteenth century.

Round-hose: short padded breeches, usually paned to show lining or other material, sixteenth century.

Shadow: woman's cap with downward point over brow and extended sides, late sixteenth–early seventeenth centuries.

Shift: woman's chemise.

Shoe-roses: rosettes decorating the fronts of shoes, late sixteenth–early seventeenth centuries.

Shoulder-rolls, wings: shoulder-decoration covering seams or points where sleeves are tied in, sixteenth–early seventeenth centuries.

Sideless gown: woman's gown open at the sides to the hips, fourteenth–fifteenth centuries.

Slashes: cuts in garments showing panes (q.v.), late fifteenth–early seventeenth centuries.

Spanish hose: calf-length breeches, not fastened at the knees, worn at a high waist-level, mid-seventeenth century.

Spoon bonnet: bonnet with crown sloped away towards the back and short flounce hanging there, 1860s.

Standing band, ruff: collar or ruff stiffened to stand upright.

Steinkirk: neckcloth put through buttonholes of coat, first half of eighteenth century.

Stole: strip of embroidered stuff shaped to put round the neck and hang down in front, worn by priests. Scarf of silk, feathers, velvet or gauze, worn by women, late eighteenth, early nineteenth centuries.

Stomacher: panel of trimmed or jewelled stuff, in form of

inverted triangle, superimposed on front of bodice, sixteenth–eighteenth centuries.

Sugar-loaf hat: tall-crowned hat with rounded top and fairly wide brim.

Surcote: outer garment, twelfth–fifteenth centuries.

Sword-carriage: straps and loops of leather depending from belt to accommodate sword.

Tabard: sleeveless outer garment with open side-seams, worn by men, mid-fifteenth century, and always by heralds.

Tippet: white linen bands with strip hanging down worn tied on above elbows, fourteenth century. Small fur necklet, seventeenth–nineteenth centuries.

Tricorne: three-cornered hat.

Trunk-hose: see 'Round-hose'.

Trunk sleeves: full sleeves diminishing towards the wrists.

Underpropper: device worn at the back of the neck to make a ruff stand upright.

Upper-stocks: name for early form of breeches, late fifteenth–early sixteenth centuries.

Venetians: breeches fastening below the knee, late sixteenth, early seventeenth centuries.

Virago sleeves: open puffed sleeves from elbow to wrist, banded by ribbons above the elbow.

Wimple: head and neck-covering, twelfth–fifteenth centuries.

CHAPTER ONE
900–1200

The beginnings of feudalism can be traced back to this period in history. Its ruling principle was the obligation of all men to their 'lord', and with the growth of a common law and central government, corresponding rights of protection. The main social elements of the kingdom were the monarch and his nobles at court, the freeman landowner, and the bondsman or serf.

The noble at court either inherited his estates or was given them by the king. Ownership gave him wealth and the privilege of being one of the king's chief advisers, but also involved an enforced duty of personal service to him. A second group of landowners comprised accountants, stewards, knights in attendance and gentleman-ushers. Some freemen farmed very small holdings of land. The status of craftsmen such as carpenters, jewellers, smiths, potters and coopers was above that of the serfs, who were allotted a strip of land and a hovel to live in and worked without pay, yielding up most of their produce in the form of taxes paid in kind.

The differences between freeman and serf were complex, and men could rise, or fall, in social status. Even a serf, however, could demand a measure of protection in case of need. This could arise from non-payment of dues, fines or taxes, from crime, debt or desertion of his land, and frequently from the question as to whether he was a serf or a freeman. The courts presided over by itinerant justices (representatives of the king) or the local magistrates were endlessly involved in litigation, seeking to prove whether an individual was free or unfree.

A freeman who was the paying tenant of a piece of land might lose this through debt or in time of war, and be forced to become an unfree land-slave. As such, he could be sold for a few shillings, or handed over, with his land, to a different lord. He might raise enough money to buy his freedom if his lord were willing, or purchase an additional strip of land, scheduled for a paying tenant, from a nearby farmer. This would make him a free landowner. If he managed to escape from his village, only a successful action in the king's court could result in his being returned to it. If he could remain for a year and a day in a chartered borough, he was free.

The strict forest laws enforced by the Normans and Plantagenets provided penalties for poaching, including fines, imprisonment, loss of freedom, even death, for taking a deer or attacking a forester. It was an offence also, to clear the wooded ground in a royal forest, or enclose its pasture for herding sheep or for agriculture. Certain rights were granted, allowing individuals to hunt fox, badger, hare, wildcat, squirrel, and wolves where they still survived.

Many towns and cities that had existed in Romano-British times had been destroyed or had fallen into ruin, since the Saxon and Danish invaders disliked and feared them. Now, new towns arose for the joint purposes of defence and trade. Castles were built for refuge and defence, and before long, every borough of any importance had one. They were also built near royal hunting-grounds, or, with the king's permission, for private ownership by noblemen.

Towns arose at cross-roads, confluences of rivers, or points at which they could be forded or bridged, and coastal havens. Markets were held in squares or streets on flat ground. Here, bargains could be concluded in public before witnesses, to avoid any later argument about ownership of property. Goods could be stored in or near a market, the mediaeval shops being chiefly workshops where orders were carried out with perhaps a few articles on view outside.

A borough held its rights by charter from the king, who often built its castle walls and ramparts. Some houses were acquired by the lords of neighbouring manors who might in their turn give the borough its charter, so that their tenants were not directly tenants of the king. The lord had access to the market for his own trade, and a house to live in when duties such as castle guard or sittings of the justiciary courts necessitated his being in town.

In England a mint and exchange for bullion existed in many boroughs by royal decree. Traders of many nations travelled easily from one country to another. Coinage was sent or carried in barrels or sacks, and could be stored in local treasuries. In the twelfth and thirteenth centuries, Jewish money-lenders would advance money at interest, a practice at first forbidden to Christians by the Church. With the persecution and expulsion of Jews from several countries, Italian money-lenders took their place and eventually became the financiers of Western Europe.

The towns represented progress, as did the gradual intake of ancient forests into cultivation. Both movements were an inevitable threat to feudalism. The boroughs were a refuge to craftsmen from serfdom. Travel between England and the Continent spread learning and new arts, as traders travelled to Scandinavia, the Baltic coast, the Rhineland markets, the cities of Italy, and the towns along the Danube.

COSTUME OF THE PERIOD: TENTH AND ELEVENTH CENTURIES

Hair—Men: In the tenth and eleventh centuries men's hair was cut to a 'bobbed' length with a centre-parting or brought forward in a fringe. In the latter case it could be graduated so that the line in profile sloped downward from the temples to the back of the head. It was sometimes allowed to grow to shoulder-length. Men of good position had their hair curled and carefully arranged. The shorter haircut of the Normans was copied by other countries, but the Norman habit of shaving the back of the head was not much followed. Late in the eleventh century long hair prevailed among Normans and other races, and continued into the twelfth century, though it did not supersede the shorter cut. Moustaches were long and drooping and beards pointed, sometimes in two or three parts.

Hair—Women: Women's hair was almost entirely covered by the headdress. Young girls could wear it loose or in two plaits, uncovered. False hair was often woven into the plaits.

Headdress—Men: The Phrygian cap in various forms, a tall conical cap and a hood with the suggestion of a peak and a shoulder-cape were the main items. Caps could be of felt, woollen material or leather.

Headdress—Women: Women wore the head-rail, a square or oblong veil. One method of putting it on was to lay it over the head with one corner hanging down in front of the left shoulder. The right-hand corner was brought across the neck under the chin and thrown over the left shoulder, and if long enough, forward again over the right. A loosely fitting hood with a shoulder-cape could be worn. The circular veil could be arranged in folds over the brow, or could have a hole made in it for the face and be used as a hood. A draped or undraped veil could be worn with a circlet to keep it in place with the longer part of the material hanging down the back. Two corners of an oblong veil could be pinned together under the chin.

Garments—Men: Men wore a basic costume of tunic or gown and a rectangular, circular or segmented cloak. Swathing or draping upward at the hips often took the place of a belt. More than one tunic could be worn for the sake of warmth. Sleeves were long and fitted to the wrists, and were made in one with the garment or set in just below the shoulders with bands of embroidery to cover the seams. The Normans introduced gowns with skirts slit from waist to hem at the sides or in front. In the latter case there was a narrow wrap-over.

The rectangular or segmented cloak was fastened on the right shoulder or at the throat with a brooch. The circular cloak had a hole to admit the face a little distance from the edge, so that only a certain amount of the cloak lay on the chest. A rectangular wrap could be draped in classical fashion over a gown.

Garments—Women: Women wore the loosely fitting three-quarter-length Saxon gown, with loose sleeves showing the close-fitting sleeves of a longer-skirted under-gown at the wrists. The outer gown was usually pouched over an unseen girdle. Its round neckline had a vertical opening in front like that of the men's tunics. This was generally worn closed and in most cases was covered by the headdress or cloak. The cloak could be circular with an opening for the face, or segmented and fastened at the throat by a brooch.

Footwear and Leg-Covering—Men: Hose made as two legs joined at the waist were worn with flat-soled shoes, soft leather boots or bootees. Leggings or bootees ending below the knees could be worn without hose.

Footwear—Women: Women wore soft flat-soled shoes or bootees of leather or fabric.

TWELFTH CENTURY

Hair—Men: Long hair was in fashion early in the century and again at the end, but in the middle years the 'bobbed' length returned. Long hair could hang loosely brushed back from the face or have two strands plaited and joined at the back. Beards and moustaches were much as before, and worn chiefly by older men.

Hair—Women: The plaiting of the hair with false hair interwoven became a more general fashion. Ornamental cases were worn covering the plaits. The hair did not show except for a little, centrally parted, over the forehead when the Norman cap and veil were worn.

Headdress—Men: The Phrygian cap and the hood were still worn. Circlets were fashionable at the beginning and end of the century. A round, head-fitting hat, with a narrow brim and a small peak on the top, and a round, flat low-crowned cap were additions.

Headdress—Women: The veil could now be very long when worn with the circlet. A dome-like cap of stiffened linen over a short veil and a wimple were worn with the clinging Norman gown. The head-rail was still in use.

Garments—Men: Gowns worn by men of important position followed Byzantine styles. The skirt of the over-gown could be draped in various ways and was often shorter than the skirt beneath. The neckline was round and decorated by a wide band of embroidery or a large circular collar. Sleeves could be moderately wide, showing close-fitting under-sleeves. They could also be long, plain and close-fitting, in some cases widening at the wrists into deep hanging cuffs, or of dolman shape, wide at the armhole and tapering to the wrists. The masculine form of the *bliaut* had a body-part swathed at the hips and a skirt of fine pleats. The tunic, lifted at the hips, remained in use unchanged. *Braccae* (trousers) were worn for active pursuits. Cloaks were as before.

Garments—Women: The unbelted clinging Norman gown and the feminine *bliaut* with its decorative corselet and pleated silk skirt were made to end just clear of the ground for practical purposes. The ordinary gown was now full-length to the instep and less voluminous than formerly. The *bliaut* could have wide pleated sleeves with close under-sleeves. All three could have sleeves widening into deep hanging cuffs at the wrists. Women of light character wore slit skirts in imitation of men.

Footwear—Men: This remained as before when worn with the tunic. With the gown, men's shoes took on varied and eccentric shapes.

Footwear—Women: Women's shoes were as in the previous centuries.

Accessories for the Tenth, Eleventh and Twelfth Centuries: Men carried spears, javelins, lances, bows and arrows, knives, swords, axes, hunting-horns and slings when dressed for warfare or hunting. Musical instruments were small harps, lyres, tabors, pipes, bassoons, cymbals and tambourines. Brooches, rings, necklaces, arm-bands, bracelets, buckles and pins, worn by men and women in Saxon dress, were made in gold, silver and bronze, sometimes set with unfaceted jewels. Pins and combs could be of bone. Decoration was in bold designs.

Materials, Colours and Ornament: Wool, leather, dressed skins and, in the latter part of the period, some cotton were used. Silk, gauze, cloth of gold and silver could be procured by the well-to-do. Colours were varied shades of blue, red, yellow, green, purple, grey, brown, black, buff and white. Ornament on dress was embroidered or applied, and in the case of the upper classes was often of gold or silver thread and sewn with jewels.

1. Anglo-Saxon Labourer

Hair: The hair is roughly cut and the short beard un-kempt.

Garments: The man wears a shirt-like garment of un-bleached linen or woollen stuff. The sleeves are rolled up.

Footwear: The feet and legs are bare.

2. Female Farm-Worker. Tenth–Eleventh Centuries.

Hair: The hair is almost hidden by the headdress.

Headdress: A hood of red wool is worn over the head and shoulders.

Garments: The under-gown is of slate-blue linen fabric with long close-fitting sleeves. It ends at the ankles and is covered by a shorter over-gown of green woollen stuff with three-quarter-length sleeves. The circular cloak of red wool has an aperture for the head, placed so that only part of it covers the chest and the remainder hangs down the back.

Footwear: Flat-soled shoes of soft brown leather are worn. They end just above the ankle-bone.

Accessories: The woman holds a primitive sort of rake con-trived of a bent piece of metal attached to a wooden staff.

3. Counsellor to an Anglo-Saxon King. Tenth–Eleventh Centuries

Hair: The hair is straight and reaches the shoulders. The beard has been cut in three points and the moustache is long and drooping.

Headdress: The tall pointed cap of black felt has a border of scarlet and green.

Garments: The old man wears a long green robe with hem and sleeve borders of black and silver and a narrow belt with silver ornaments. His red cloak is fastened in front with a large brooch. It is lined with black and has a border of yellow and black.

Shoes: The ornate shoes are of red leather ornamented in black and silver.

Accessories: The counsellor holds a staff and a rolled-up scroll of parchment.

4. Anglo-Saxon Youth. Tenth–Eleventh Centuries

Hair: The boy's curled hair is cut to a 'bobbed' length.

Garments: The tunic has a round neckline and long close-fitting sleeves. The bodice is swathed at the hips over an unseen belt. The skirt is draped so that the hem dips at the sides. The garment is of yellow wool, with embroidery in mid-blue woollen thread.

Hose: The yellow woollen hose end below the knees and are bordered with blue woollen embroidery.

Shoes: The flat-soled bootees are of scarlet leather.

Accessories: The boy holds a metal rod and a bowl with meat in it. He has speared some of this with the rod and is about to pass it to his master, who will draw it off the rod with his hand. The youth will kneel to offer it.

5. Anglo-Saxon Spearman. Tenth–Eleventh Centuries

Hair: The man's hair is of 'bobbed' length.

Headdress: The brown felt Phrygian cap has a small peak and an ornamented border of red and yellow.

Garments: The tunic is of light-brown woollen stuff with scarlet and yellow ornament. It has a round neckline and long plain sleeves. Its skirts have been replaced by loose breeches, with an embroidered border all round the edges in the same colours as those at the neck and wrists. The large rectangular cloak is of dark-red wool, held together on the right shoulder by a metal ring.

Shoes: The bootees of brown leather are laced on the outside of the leg and come up to the base of the calf. They are turned over at the top.

Accessories: The man carries a spear and a hunting-horn.

6. Anglo-Saxon Bowman. Tenth–Eleventh Centuries

Hair: The hair is long and straight, parted from front to back in the centre, with the strands tied together behind each ear and ending below the shoulders. The moustache is long and drooping and the beard pointed.

Garments: The man wears a tunic in dull green with a yellow-patterned border to the round neckline. This is repeated at the wrists, at the hem, the open sides of the skirt and across the top of the skirt where there is an apron-like strip of material. The belt is covered by the folds of the tunic. The small circular or oval cloak has an opening in its centre for the head and is of brown woollen fabric. It hangs down in folds of equal depth over the chest and back. These are drawn together by a circular brooch on each shoulder.

Boots: The man wears calf-length boots of soft wrinkled brown leather, made higher at the back than at the front. The part covering the foot is in the form of a bootee, attached to the top by an ornamented border. His knees and the upper part of his legs are bare.

Accessories: He carries a bow and arrow.

7. Anglo-Saxon Peasant. Tenth–Eleventh Centuries

Hair: The hair is brought forward from the crown of the head on to the forehead and is 'bobbed' all round, left longer at the back than at the sides.

Garments: The man wears two tattered tunics, one over the other, of brown and buff-yellow respectively. The over-tunic is pouched slightly over the belt, which is un-seen, and is pulled up here and there so that it hangs unevenly.

Hose: The clumsy hose of unbleached linen have green cross-bindings.

Shoes: The soft flat shoes are of brown leather.

Accessories: The man carries a club and a lantern to which a piece of rope is attached.

8. Welsh Warrior. Tenth–Eleventh Centuries

Hair: The hair is worn fairly long and straight.

Headdress: The man wears a version of the Phrygian cap in red felt.

Garments: The close-fitting tunic, ending at the hips, is of 'rayed' material in scarlet and the natural colour of wool. The braccae (trousers) match this and the girdle, knotted in front, is of scarlet padded linen or woollen stuff.

Shoes: These are of red leather and end just below the ankle-bone.

Accessories: The man carries a short wooden lance, curved because it comes from the bough of a tree, with an iron head.

9. Man and Blind Girl. Beggars. Tenth–Eleventh Centuries

Hair: The girl's unkempt hair hangs loosely. The man's hair, beard and moustache are raggedly cut.

Headdress: The girl has a rectangular cloth over her head and a loose bandage covering her right eye.

Garments: The girl wears part of a torn gown and has a ragged length of stuff in faded neutral colours wound round her as a garment. The man wears a tattered dun-coloured tunic which the girl is holding to guide her steps.

Footwear: The girl's legs and feet (unseen) are bare. The man's are also bare except for a bandage round one leg.

Accessories: The girl carries a begging-bowl. The man cannot stand and has wooden contrivances like small trestles which he grasps in his hands and moves in front of him to drag himself along the ground.

10. Girl with Spindle and Thread. Eleventh–Twelfth Centuries

Hair: The hair is hidden by the head-rail.

Headdress: A Saxon head-rail of pale-green wool is laid over the head with two folds made at a diagonal and the ends are folded, one from left to right over the right shoulder, and the other from right to left over the left shoulder.

Garments: The plain dun-coloured gown has a girdle at the hips, over which some folds are bloused, and comes to the ankles. It has long over-sleeves, showing part of the dark-green sleeves of an under-tunic.

Shoes: The bootees have flat soles and are of grey fabric.

Accessories: The girl holds a large spindle and a bobbin with thread.

11. Administrator to a Nobleman. Eleventh–Twelfth Centuries

Hair: The hair is curled and comes down to the shoulders. The beard is cut in two long points.

Headdress: The man wears a Phrygian cap with an elongated peak. It is of green felt or leather, with ornament of silver braid and purple unfaceted stones.

Garments: The gown ends above the ankles, and is of grey-green silken fabric with applied ornaments in an all-over pattern of dull silver, and a border to the neckline, sleeves and hem in silver and purple. The over-sleeves are of three-quarter length, showing part of the close-fitting sleeves of a dull purple under-tunic. The long rectangular drapery of fine purple wool, worn over the gown, is put on as follows: Tie a cord round the waist and drop one end of the wrap forward over the right shoulder, leaving some to hang down at the back. Bring this length across the back to the left side, then by twisting and rolling this length at the top edge, tuck it into the waist-cord and take it all round the body, letting some of the width of the material droop downwards.

Hose: These are grey-green and cover the legs beneath the gown.

Bootees: The green leather bootees are decorated with silver thread.

12. Norman Woodcutter. Eleventh–Twelfth Centuries

Hair: A lock of hair comes forward on the right side of the forehead. The whole of the back of the head is shaved.

Garments: The short tunic of rust-red cloth has a vertical opening at the front of the neck and long close-fitting sleeves. It is tucked into the belt of the breeches. The ornament at cuffs and neckline is in green and dark brown. The rust-coloured loose breeches have a decorative border of wool embroidery in orange and green, and a matching belt.

Hose: The hose are of light-brown yarn.

Shoes: The brown leather shoes have turnovers at the front and back of the ankles.

13. Major-Domo or Steward of a Nobleman's House. Eleventh–Twelfth Centuries

Hair: The hair is curled and descends to the nape of the neck at the back, while a lock is arranged to droop over the forehead. Some of the hair at the sides of the forehead has been shaved.

Garments: The pale-coral-coloured gown has long close sleeves and a round neckline. In addition to embroidery in scarlet and silver at the neck and wrists, motifs of similar ornament decorate the shoulders and forearms. The gown is open at the right side of the front from waist to hem, and is bordered with the scarlet and silver embroidery.

Hose: The long parchment-coloured hose are made as two separate legs joined at the waist.

Shoes: The shoes are of scarlet leather ornamented in silver.

Accessories: The steward is filling a goblet with wine from a pottery jug which stands on a small stone pedestal.

14. Woman in Large Circular Cloak. Eleventh–Twelfth Centuries

Hair: This is hidden by the headdress.

Headdress: A green woollen head-rail is worn over a stiffened cap of unbleached linen.

Garments: The over-gown is of deep-green woollen stuff with a border in dark red and black. It ends at calf-level, showing part of the skirt of a dark-red under-gown. The left sleeve of the over-gown has been brought down to cover the hand for warmth. The large thick circular cloak of brownish-grey wool is pulled up over the left shoulder to free the left arm and on the other side covers the right hand.

Shoes: Black leather shoes with flat soles are worn and the feet are raised on clogs with straps over the insteps.

Accessories: The woman, probably a farmer's wife, carries a walking-stick.

15. Young Waiting-Gentlewoman or Daughter of the House. Late Eleventh–Twelfth Centuries

Hair: The hair is parted in the centre and wound into two long plaits to which false hair has been added.

Headdress: Silver ribbons have been twined into the plaits.

Garments: The girl wears a gown of scarlet silk which clings to the figure and touches the ground at the hem. It has been lifted at the sides to create some folds in front. It has a round neckline ornamented in silver, and the right sleeve has the deep cuff of Norman fashion. Its end has been knotted to keep it out of the way and the left sleeve shortened for greater freedom of movement, leaving the forearm bare. The under-gown is either not worn or its sleeve has been rolled back.

Shoes: The flat slippers are of scarlet leather.

Accessories: A silver bowl of fruit is carried. Dishes of this type were set along the tables.

16. Male Dancer (Member of a Minstrel Troupe). Twelfth Century

Hair: The young man's hair is curled and cut fairly short.

Garments: The tunic has a round neckline and dolman sleeves. Its skirt is draped upward at the hips, creating an apron effect in front. It is of white silk, with embroidery in crimson, silver and dull pink.

Hose: The white hose are made as two separate legs, joined at the top.

Shoes: These are of crimson fabric with silver fastenings.

17. French Housewife. Twelfth Century

Hair: This is hidden by the headdress.

Headdress: The white linen hood is not wrapped round the neck but is worn open. It is put on over a stiffened foundation that gives it a slightly high crown.

Garments: The woman wears a gown of coarse green-grey linen with a V-shaped opening at the neck (usually hidden by the hood) and a swathed belt of the same stuff as the dress. The dress ends just clear of the ground. The long sleeves widen near the wrists and have deep pendent cuffs in the Norman fashion.

Shoes: These are of fabric and follow a Norman fashion in the pointed toes.

Accessories: The woman is carrying a pottery jug.

18. Waiting Gentlewoman in Modified *Bliaut*. Twelfth Century

Hair: The girl's natural hair is parted in the centre and bound with some false hair in two long twists, fastened together by ribbon with gilt casing and tassels at the ends.

Headdress: She wears a small shallow circular cap of deep-blue felt, set on the crown of the head.

Garments: The dress is of brilliant blue silk embroidered at the neck, bosom and sleeve-ends in gold and deeper blue. The corset-like over-bodice is of gold tissue and its girdle is ornamented in the same way as the dress. It is tied with gold cord and tassels. The outer sleeves have deep cuffs lengthening abruptly at the wrists in the Norman fashion. These are knotted at the ends to keep them out of the way. The inner sleeves are of gold tissue. The crinkled and pleated skirt ends at the instep. This is a modification of the original flowing skirt of the *bliaut*.

Shoes: The flat slippers are of gold cloth sewn with jewels.

Accessories: The girl has brought a mirror and a jar of unguent or cosmetic to her lady.

19. Girl Entertainer. Twelfth Century

Hair: The hair is left to hang loosely over the shoulders.

Headdress: The girl wears a shallow Phrygian cap of scarlet felt with a border of gold embroidery.

Garments: The white silk under-tunic has three-quarter length close-fitting sleeves embroidered in gold at the ends. The skirt is open in front in imitation of a masculine fashion. Over it is worn a close-fitting tunic of gilt leather scales. It ends at the hips and has short shoulder-pieces instead of sleeves. The collar, belt and border are of gilt leather set with glass jewels and edged with scarlet.

Hose: The scarlet hose are decorated down the front with unfaceted glass ornaments in green, red, blue and yellow.

Accessories: The girl holds an unfolded scroll.

20. Housewife or Waiting-Woman with Candlestick. Twelfth Century

Hair: The hair is parted in the centre and is almost covered by the headdress.

Headdress: The straight edge of the semicircular grey cloak is draped over the head and the two sides caught together at the throat by a brooch.

Garments: The woman wears an instep-length dress of violet wool with three-quarter length sleeves showing the dark red sleeves of the under-gown. Decoration of dark red and silver edges the sleeves and hem of the gown and also ornaments the belt.

Shoes: Flat slippers of dark-red fabric with silver ornament are worn.

Accessories: The tall silver candlestick is of the type often used to stand on the floor. The candle is fixed on to a metal prong at the top of the candlestick.

21. Harper in a Nobleman's House. Twelfth Century

Hair: The hair is long, reaching the shoulders. A moustache and beard are worn.

Headdress: The harper wears a gold circlet on his head.

Garments: The long robe, a form of *bliaut*, is of heavy ivory silk, decorated at the wrists and hem in scarlet, black and green, and with a large circular collar in the same colours. It is draped upward at the hips over an under-gown.

Shoes: The scarlet leather shoes have flat soles.

Accessories: The man is playing a small harp.

22. Serving-Maid. Twelfth Century

Hair: The hair is cut in a fringe in front and hangs down over the shoulders.

Headdress: The round cap is of dark-red felt with a border of buff-yellow and a gold ornament on the top.

Garments: The girl wears a long-sleeved gown of wine-coloured woollen stuff, without an over-gown. It is drawn in at a rather high waistline and has a hood of buff-yellow woollen fabric thrown back on the shoulders. A panel of buff-yellow with decoration embroidered on it in dull gold is attached to the front of the dress from the waist to a point at calf-level, where a deep band of the same stuff forms the lower part of the skirt. The top of the white chemise can be seen. The costume shows a definite Byzantine origin.

Footwear: The flat slippers, scarcely seen, are of dark-red leather.

Accessories: She carries a silver casket or reliquary.

23. Girl in Knotted Veil. Twelfth Century

Hair: The hair shows only in front. It is parted in the centre and smoothed down on either side of the temples.

Headdress: The long rectangular veil of thin ivory-white silk is put over the head and knotted at the right side of the neck towards the back. The ends are brought round to the front over the left shoulder.

Garments: The clinging gown of pale turquoise-blue silk touches the floor and has long close-fitting sleeves. Over it is worn a circular or oval cloak with an opening for the head nearer to the edge than the central point, so that only a part of it falls over the chest. It is of pale coral-coloured silk with gold decoration.

Shoes: Flat slippers of gilt leather are worn.

Accessories: The girl carries a covered silver vessel containing heated wine or a hot medicinal cordial, and is using one end of her veil to protect her hands. She wears a gold ornament at the neck of her dress.

24. Shepherd. Late Twelfth Century

Hair: This is visible in front, in strands over his forehead.

Headdress: The brown woollen hood has a short *liripipe* and a large shoulder-cape coming well down over the shoulders.

Garments: The long unbelted surcote ending below the calves is of rough sage-green frieze. It is slit in front for freedom of movement and has loose sleeves showing the tight sleeves of the dark-brown under-tunic at the wrists.

Hose: The hose are of coarse grey yarn.

Boots: Short clumsy bootees of black leather are worn.

Accessories: The shepherd carries a sheep-crook.

25. Woman Feeding Doves. Late Twelfth Century

Hair: This is almost hidden by the headdress, but shows a little in front, parted in the centre.

Headdress: The white veil of finely woven linen, silk or wool is laid over the head, fastened to the hair at the temples, and covers the shoulders.

Garments: The over-dress of fine pale-blue wool hangs loosely to the hem from a close round neckline and trails on the ground. It has three-quarter length sleeves of moderate width, showing part of the close-fitting sleeves of a silver-grey under-gown. The cloak is of sapphire-blue woollen fabric, made in an oval shape and drawn together at the base of the throat by a jewelled brooch.

Shoes: The flat slippers of blue fabric are hardly seen.

Accessories: The woman carries a shallow bowl of grain for feeding her doves.

CHAPTER TWO
1200–1380

The opening up of new trade-routes as a result of the Crusaders' journeys, and the re-establishment of old ones, meant an increase of commerce with the Near East. Guilds and corporations were formed in trading circles, and cities prospered as goods were transported by land and water. Lemons, oranges, grapes and wine were imported from the Mediterranean countries, also figs, cucumbers, melons, aloes, pepper, cardamoms and cloves; soap and oil came from Nablus, carpets from Tiberias, pottery and glass from Tyre, silk from Antioch and cotton from Tripoli; and from the Northern countries, pitch, wax, copper, herrings and salt-fish. English exports were wool, cloth, corn, barley, leather, iron, lead, tin, horses and cattle. After Marco Polo's explorations, towards the end of the thirteenth century, trade routes to the Far East were opened up and Europe received cargoes of magnificent silks, jewels, velvet and furs, and Oriental spices.

The discoveries and inventions of the early Renaissance brought a new flowering of knowledge, and of skills hitherto lost or unknown in Western Europe. The rudder for ships and the marine compass in a primitive form (a device already known in the past to Arab conquerors through the Greeks) gave to sailors safer and more speedy means of navigation. The development of the optic lens brought the magnifying-glass into use, also framed spectacles, without side-pieces. The use of the windmill and the wheelbarrow began in this period. The rigid yoke, the iron shoe (already discovered earlier in Byzantium) and the breast-strap made the horse, which had been used chiefly for riding, into a more useful animal for ploughing and draught purposes.

In dwelling-houses chimneys were beginning to take the place of the hole in the roof and the fire in the centre of the room. Rushes were still laid on the floor, but some wealthy families had small carpets, following a fashion brought to Spain by the Moors. Rooms were better furnished than in earlier times, with tables, stools, settles and coffers of oak or pine. Chairs were few, but square or circular cushions and narrow mattresses filled with flock or feathers made for comfort on the hard surfaces of the sparse furniture. Only in the conditions of the very poor was there no improvement, and it was to be many centuries before their homes were better than hovels.

In richer houses, beds were usually four-posters with canopies, valances and curtains of rich materials. In the daytime a room holding a bed of this kind became a living room in which the master and mistress of a house could spend their leisure and receive their guests. Often a truckle-bed, low enough to be wheeled out of sight beneath the great bed, was kept in the room for a child or a servant sleeping there. Children, pages, servants and knights in attendance on their lord slept on straw pallets, no definite sleeping-quarters being provided for them until much later.

In the fourteenth century tapestries and wall-hangings of silk, velvet, damask and fine wool, woven or embroidered with gold or silver thread, covered brightly painted walls, and, with furniture also painted, a brilliant effect was achieved.

The castle with its keep had surrounding walls of stone, and usually a moat or drawbridge. It was unusual for it to be lived in continually, as its primary function was one of defence. A manor-house was often built adjacent to it or within its precincts. Unfortified houses were still built largely of clay, rubble and plaster, with supports of timber and a tiled or thatched roof. Some stone was used for semi-fortification.

The mediaeval manor or castle kept open house for travellers and sheltered those who needed charity. Until the late fourteenth century the feudal lord dined with his household and guests in the Great Hall. At banquets many courses of meat and game were served, with rich sauces accompanied by bread. Elaborate sweetmeats were brought to the table between meat courses, and entertainment was provided by minstrels and dancers.

Kings and noblemen used to move from one estate to another for the purpose of checking on taxation. Their numerous military retainers set up armed camps along the routes and in some cases pillaged the countryside. The muddy, uneven highways were crowded with this traffic and with the passage of farmers taking beasts to market, pedlars, strolling players and minstrels, fugitives from outbreaks of plague, beggars and wandering friars. These religious mendicants travelled long distances on horse, mule or foot, bringing news as well as ministration to illiterate people in isolated places and preaching in towns and villages.

By lesser-known byways and forest paths, avoiding the populous highroads, men sought a way to liberty from serfdom in villages whose population of male workers had been decimated by plague or by migration to towns. Those who failed to find employment as labourers or craftsmen were reduced to the life of outlaws, and many became criminals.

Many of the principal officers of State, such as treasurers, ambassadors and chancellors, were bishops and cardinals. As a result, these bishops neglected their pastoral duties, and the ministry in parish churches often fell into the hands of incompetent priests, and even laymen if the gift of a living was in lay hands. The monasteries grew wealthy through endowments, tithes and acquisition of land and treasure. The monks gave up the manual labour enjoined on their predecessors and employed servants. They abandoned their habits for ordinary dress to hunt or travel for pleasure, and besides carrying out the normal duties of giving alms daily, feeding the hungry and saying prayers and masses for living and dead, they welcomed as guests influential and wealthy patrons.

In this period of partial disrepute in the ordinary service of religion, a large part of the enormous wealth acquired by the Church, the nobility and the merchant classes was used for the building of magnificent cathedrals, churches, abbeys and chantries.

COSTUME OF THE PERIOD: THIRTEENTH CENTURY

Hair—Men: The hair could have a centre-parting or be brought forward unparted in a fringe. Another fashion was to part it across the front of the head and brush the front length back in a curled roll or turn it under in a roll over the forehead. Men could be clean-shaven or bearded. Moustaches were worn with beards, but not alone.

Hair—Women: Plaits or coils over the ears or across the head were worn, or the hair could be put up in a low chignon. Young girls might wear it hanging loose.

Headdress—Men: Headgear worn by itself or covered by a hat included: the white or black coif (a plain linen cap fitting the head and tied under the chin); the hood, which usually had a deep round shoulder-cape and a peak or a *liripipe*, short at first, but lengthening during the century; and occasionally the *barbette* (see 'Headdress—Women'). Other forms of headdress were: a soft-crowned cap with a narrow upturned brim and, as a rule, a small tag on the top; a saucepan-shaped hat with a decorated rim and a plain, almost flat crown; a narrower pill-box shape; a version of the Phrygian cap with a long peak back and front; a round, head-fitting cap with a narrow upturned brim, and one with a flattened top and no brim. Late in the century a hat with a wide brim, often turned up all round, was in fashion.

Headdress—Women: The following could be worn with caps of various shapes, turned back from the face, or with the short rectangular veil called the *couvrechef*: the head-rail of earlier times; the *barbette*, a chin-band put on under the jaw and fastened near the top of the head with the widest part covering the ears; the hood, with a peak or short *liripipe*; the wimple, a hood without a peak, covering the neck and the back of the head; the *gorget*, in reality the wimple pulled down to uncover the top of the head and fastened to coils of hair over the ears, and the *ramshorn*, a length of material laid across the top and back of the head, with its ends wrapped round coils of hair on each side; pill-box and saucepan-shaped caps like those of men, and a shallow hat with a turned-down brim introduced late in the century. Jewelled or beaded nets confined the chignon. Young girls might crown their unbound hair with wreaths. Circlets could surmount pill-box caps when worn by women of high position.

Garments—Men: The chief garments worn by men were: a tunic ending at or above the knees; a loose or belted gown with moderately wide sleeves, showing the close-fitting sleeves of an under-tunic and ending at the ankle or instep; a loosely hanging surcote with a slit in the front and often the sides of the skirt, also ending at the ankle or instep; a belted cote with draped shoulders and plain or dolman sleeves, with skirt slit from waist to hem in front and worn over full breeches tied beneath the knees; a similar garment worn over a knee-length tunic with the slit lower down; and late in the century a sleeveless *cyclas*, long or three-quarter length, worn over a tunic with plain or dolman sleeves or sleeves full to the elbow and tight-fitting from elbow to wrist.

Outer garments were the long or three-quarter length *ganache*, a loose gown with the sleeves contrived by leaving the side-seems open from shoulder to hip; and the *hérigault*, a similar gown with cape sleeves pleated vertically at the shoulders. Long circular and semi-circular cloaks were worn.

These costumes were worn by men of most classes and occupations, differentiated by the cut and quality of material. Exceptions were the third type of sleeve worn with the *cyclas* and the pleated sleeves of the *hérigault*. These were worn by the nobility, architects, physicians, merchants and other men of good position.

Garments—Women: Women's gowns were long and flowing and were with difficulty pinned up or partially shortened for practical work.

A straight, unbelted gown falling in long folds from shoulder to hem; the twelfth-century gown, slightly shaped to the body, in the early part of the century, and one with the upper part bloused over a belt were the main garments at the opening of the period. A gown with a more closely fitting upper part and a downward-pointing belt was added later. Long cloaks like those of men were worn.

Hose–Men: Hose were now usually joined at the waist and had leather soles attached for wearing without shoes. Some cross-binding was seen.

Footwear—Men: Shoes and bootees slightly pointed but following the shape of the foot were worn. They often came up to the ankle-bone and were plain or decorated according to the wearer's status.

Hose—Women: Women are thought to have worn hose gartered at the knee.

Shoes—Women: Women's shoes were like those of men.

Materials, Colour and Ornament: Wool, linen and some cotton were the stuffs mainly used for practical dress. Vivid colours such as scarlet, crimson, blue, yellow, purple, orange, red-brown, green and a deep pink were worn, as well as duller tints which included brown, grey, russet, black, brown-purple and slate-blue. Contrasting shades might be worn together. Circlets and jewelled belts were worn by people of good position.

FOURTEENTH CENTURY

Hair—Men: Worn as in the thirteenth century. It could be brushed loosely back unparted. Moustaches could be small, meeting short fringe beards, or drooping with a single, bifid or trifid beard.

Hair—Women: Women pinned the hair up in coils or plaits at the sides of the head. Young girls could wear it loose.

Headdress—Men: The coif, hood and hats of the thirteenth century remained in use. The *liripipe* could be wound round the hood, and a hat called the *chaperon* was developed from it. The saucepan-shaped hat could have a *couvrechef* thrown over it. A hat turned up at the back, with a long peak in front, was worn sideways or back to front. Many soft or stiff-crowned caps were in use.

Headdress—Women: The head-rail was still used with practical dress. The gorget was in fashion during the first thirty years. The peaked hat worn by men was put on over the wimple. The saucepan-shaped hat was widened to accommodate side-plaits. The *couvrechef* was worn over this and over the reticulated headdress, an arrangement of wire, silk and jewelled or beaded nets. Wreaths of real or artificial flowers and velvet rondels were worn. From about 1350 the horseshoe-shaped *nebulae* headdress of wired gauze was in fashion for about thirty years. A circlet could be worn with side-plaits pinned over it.

Garments—Men: Features of the period were: the loosely fitting surcote of the thirteenth century, and knee-length tunics with the skirt draped upward at one side in the first thirty years; from the second quarter the *cotehardie*, a body-fitting garment ending at the knee, calf or instep with long close sleeves, and a figure-fitting surcote with long tight sleeves and slits in the skirt ending at the calf. A hood-collar with a shoulder-cape was worn with this and with the *cotehardie*. A short *cotehardie* with the belt set low was in vogue in the second part of the century. The innovation of the garment known as the *houppeland* is described in the next chapter.

Garments—Women: The loosely fitting *cyclas* and similar gowns were worn in the first quarter of the century. The feminine version of the *cotehardie* that followed fitted the figure and had an oval neckline and long close sleeves. The sideless dress which came in about 1330 was open to the hips and was worn over a *cotehardie*. The flowing skirts of these gowns could be made in a shorter and more manageable form for active work.

Hose—Men: These were the same as in the preceding century, except that cross-binding was not worn. Long complete hose with leather soles were often worn instead of shoes and were frequently parti-coloured.

Hose—Women: Women's hose were the same as in the preceding century.

Shoes—Men: Long pointed toes to shoes and bootees came in early in the century. More normal shapes were worn for practical reasons or for preference.

Shoes—Women: These resembled those of men.

Materials, Colour and Ornament: Colours and stuffs were much as in the thirteenth century, but a good deal of parti-coloured and heraldic dress was worn, and dagged edges were fashionable.

26. Falconer in Hooded Cape (a Spanish Fashion). Early Thirteenth Century

Hair: This is almost entirely concealed by the hood.

Headdress: The hood is made in one with the outer wrap and has a short *liripipe* hanging from the crown of the head.

Garments: The tunic is of flame-coloured silk, with a pattern of gold thread and pale-yellow trefoil motifs. Only part of the right sleeve can be seen. The outer garment of rose-tan cloth is made like a wide-skirted sleeveless coat, with deep openings for the armholes. A short cape is made in one with it. The fastening is down the front, from beneath the chin to the hem.

Hose: Dark copper-coloured hose with leather soles are worn.

Accessories: The man wears natural leather gauntlet-gloves with gilt ornaments on the backs, and carries a young kite on his left hand.

27. Man with Scythe. Thirteenth Century

Hair: The hair is roughly cut in a 'bobbed' shape.

Headdress: The battered hat is of natural straw.

Garments: The man wears a voluminous loin-cloth of natural-coloured wool or linen.

Feet: His feet are bare.

28. Huntsman. Thirteenth Century

Hair: The hair is curled and has been brushed upward over the front of the cap. It also shows below it at the back.

Headdress: A white linen coif is tied under the chin.

Garments: The huntsman wears breeches of bright-red wool below his tunic. These are fairly full in cut and are tied below the knees. The tunic is of the same colour and is made with a draped neck and shoulder-line and narrow close-fitting sleeves. It is open in front from waist to hem and ends at calf-level.

Hose: The hose are red.

Boots: The bootees are of black buckskin and end above the ankles.

Accessories: The huntsman carries a knife, with the sheath hung from his belt, and a hunting-horn on a strap round his neck.

29. Housewife or Waiting-Woman with Ewer and Basin. Thirteenth Century (German Fashion)

Hair: This is hidden by the headdress.

Headdress: A white linen barbette is put on beneath the chin and fastened on the top of the head. A flat-topped white linen cap is worn over it.

Garments: The woman wears a gown of deep-orange wool, of a length that touches the floor. Over it is worn a tabard-shaped over-gown of mushroom-brown woollen stuff. It has shoulder-pieces in place of sleeves and the sides are open, except that they are caught together under the arms.

Shoes: The flat slippers of brown fabric are hardly seen.

Accessories: The woman carries a ewer and basin of copper, pewter or silver.

30. Man with Spade. Thirteenth Century

Hair: The man's roughly cut hair hangs down beneath his cap. He has a fringe beard and thin moustache.

Headdress: The round flat-topped cap is of red felt bordered with black.

Garments: The labourer wears a pair of braccae (trousers) of natural-coloured wool or unbleached linen. The top of these is rolled over a waist-cord.

Footwear: The shoes are flat-soled, of brown leather or fabric, fastening down the front of the instep.

Accessories: The man is using the spade with a pointed blade and long haft usual in mediaeval times.

31. Man Travelling the Roads. Late Thirteenth Century

Hair: The man's curly hair comes forward in a large quiff over the forehead. He wears a beard and moustache.

Headdress: The fawn-coloured felt hat has a soft crown and a circular brim turned up all round. It is worn over a dark-green woollen hood with a shoulder-cape.

Garments: The close-fitting sleeves of a fawn-coloured under-tunic are seen at the wrists. The brick-red woollen gown ends at the calves and has three-quarter length sleeves. A shorter loosely fitting garment known as a *ganache* is worn over this. It has an opening for the head with small oval lapels. The sleeves are contrived by leaving part of the side-seams open below the shoulders to admit the arms and closing them again at the hips. It is of dark-green woollen stuff, lined with lighter green.

Hose: The hose are of coarse grey yarn.

Boots: Short bootees of brown buckskin are worn.

Accessories: The man holds a crook-handled stick over his shoulder on which are hung a cloak or blanket and a small cooking vessel. He carries a basket of crockery and personal belongings in the other hand.

32. Girl with Covered Jug. Late Thirteenth Century

Hair: The hair is parted in the centre and coiled at the back of the neck.

Headdress: A snood of sapphire-blue mesh lined with red silk is worn.

Garments: The girl wears an under-gown of slate-blue loosely woven linen with scarlet fringe, of which only the hem can be seen in front. Over it is a gown of sapphire-blue wool with long close-fitting sleeves. Its skirt is fastened up at intervals in front to give freedom in walking and the back breadth turned up and fastened at the back of the waist to the under-gown. The pale-grey lining can be seen. Over these is a scarlet *cyclas* of thin wool, turned up like the gown, showing a pinkish-red lining, and fastened to the gown at the back of the waist.

Footwear: Flat slippers of red leather or fabric are worn.

Accessories: The girl carries a covered wine-jug of silver or other metal.

33. Female Dancer (Member of a Minstrel Troupe). Late Thirteenth Century

Hair: The hair is wound into twists or plaits over the ears.

Headdress: A silver net lined with scarlet, with side-pieces to cover the twists of hair over the ears, covers the head as well.

Garments: The dancer wears a blue woollen dress with a round neckline, a moderately fitted bodice belted at the waist, and dolman sleeves. The skirt is long and very full, probably allowing only for slow posturing. The belt and the decoration at the neck are of scarlet and silver.

Shoes: The shoes are of blue fabric with scarlet ornaments.

34. *Châtelaine* or Waiting-Gentlewoman. Early Fourteenth Century

Hair: A little hair shows at the temples and at the back of the neck.

Headdress: The white linen headdress is formed of a cap turned back from the face, with lappets arranged at the sides and back.

Garments: The under-gown of red, gold and black is turned up in front to facilitate movement. The gown of soft pearl-grey wool is very long and its flowing skirts are held up in the crook of the left arm against the body. It is belted at the waist and has long, close-fitting sleeves. The shortening of the under-gown gives little help in managing the dress as this must still be lifted on the arms. The large semicircular cloak of dark-red cloth has a hood thrown back on the shoulders and is lined with fur.

Shoes: Flat-soled slippers of red leather are worn.

Accessories: The woman holds a goblet in one hand and a pewter or silver double-handled jug in the other. She is offering wine to travellers or guests, who are arriving or departing from a castle.

35. Gentleman-Servitor. Early Fourteenth Century

Hair: The hair is cut in a rounded shape, fairly short, and is brought forward in front from the crown of the head to the brow.

Headdress: A small wreath of pink flowers in enamel and gilt jeweller's work is worn high on the head.

Garments: The gown ends above the ankles and is of pinkish-orange silk with dolman sleeves to the wrists. The close-fitting rounded neckline is edged with sherry-brown silk and an under-tunic of the same stuff shows a little where the skirt of the gown is slit in front.

Hose: The hose are of a brownish neutral shade.

Shoes: The shoes, of brown fabric, end at the ankle-bones.

Accessories: A long narrow scarf of finely woven white linen is wound about the body and is used to wipe crockery or hand hot dishes. The man carries a slim-necked pottery vessel.

36. Major-Domo or Steward to a Nobleman. Early Fourteenth Century

Hair: The man's hair is curled and hangs down over the collar from a centre-parting. He has a long drooping moustache and a pointed beard.

Garments: He wears a tunic of calf-length in heavy pale-blue silk with decoration in scarlet and gold. It has long close-fitting sleeves and a belt of scarlet and gold plaques. Over it is a cloak with a high collar, fastened on the right shoulder, of fine scarlet cloth. It has a border of gold braid studded with unfaceted imitation jewels.

Hose: The pale-blue hose match the tunic.

Shoes: The shoes are of scarlet and gold leather.

Accessories: The steward carries a wand of office.

37. Young Servant in Belted Gown. Early Fourteenth Century

Hair: The hair is cut to a 'bobbed' length.

Headdress: The brown cap is circular and brimless, with a small tag on the pointed top, and is made of a stretching material, possibly knitted.

Garments: The youth wears an under-tunic of dark-green cloth which ends at the calf and has long close-fitting sleeves. Over it is a *cyclas* of copper-coloured woollen stuff. This has a round neckline and is decorated with buttons down the front. It has no sleeves and the deep armholes extend to the waist. In this instance it is worn with a brown leather belt.

Hose: The dark-green hose have leather soles.

Accessories: The boy is holding his master's yellow linen under-tunic, which has long plain sleeves and a circular neckline with a vertical opening at the throat. A brown leather pouch is attached to his belt.

38. German Nobleman in the Capacity of a Judge. Early Fourteenth Century

Hair: The hair is worn in a fringe over the forehead and is cut in a 'bobbed' shape at the back and sides, covering the ears.

Headdress: The judge wears the ducal crown of red velvet and gold.

Garments: The surcote is of darkish blue silk with a narrow gold border at the neck (unseen), ends of the outer sleeves, the hem and the edges of the slit in the front of the gown. The sleeves of the under-gown are green. Over this is a cloak of red velvet lined with white fur. It has a deep shoulder-cape decorated with the same fur.

Shoes: The shoes of black velvet have moderate points and are bordered in white where they end at the ankles.

Accessories: The judge carries a sheathed sword with his belt wound round it as a symbol of Justice. At this time the law in many criminal cases was administered by noblemen and clerics.

39. Gentleman-Servitor Travelling with his Master. Early Fourteenth Century

Hair: The hair is unseen except where it shows at the back beneath the coif.

Headdress: The cap of fluted yellow stiffened fabric with a top of dark blue is worn over a yellow linen coif.

Garments: The surcote is of finely woven pale-yellow cloth, bordered at the neck, outer sleeve-ends and hem in silver, dark blue, yellow and pale green. The cloak of dark-blue velvet is fastened across the chest by silver bars with a silver brooch each side and is lined with silver-grey silk. The buckled belt is in the same colours as the ornament on the gown.

Hose: The hose are pale grey.

Boots: The bootees are of grey leather, open over half the insteps and fastening on the outer sides of the ankles with silver buttons. They are studded with small silver ornaments.

Accessories: The servitor is travelling with his lord on a progress through his estates and gives him personal service such as putting food and drink before him. He is bringing him a bowl of broth.

40. Youth Sowing Grain. Early Fourteenth Century

Hair: The 'bobbed' hair is of moderate length.

Headdress: The youth wears a yellow linen *barbette*, fastened under the chin and surmounted by a flat circular or oval cap of matching felt which is attached to the *barbette*.

Garments: The stuff of the tunic is woven in broad horizontal stripes of pale leaf-green and mushroom-brown. The neckline forms a straight line across the collar-bones; the sleeves are of dolman shape. The front breadth of the skirt is draped upward on the left side and tucked into the belt. Beneath it loose breeches of matching green are worn, ending above the knees.

Hose: The long hose match the brown of the tunic.

Shoes: The ankle-strapped shoes are of brown leather.

Accessories: A canvas bag is slung across the youth's left shoulder and he is throwing grain from it into the ground.

41. Peasant Woman. Fourteenth Century

Hair: A little shows in a ragged fringe over the forehead.

Headdress: The hood of pale fawn-coloured wool has a shoulder-cape and a short *liripipe* hanging down at the back.

Garments: The woman wears a dun-coloured woollen gown with plain long sleeves. Over it is a dark-maroon open-sided dress and an apron of coarse natural linen, smocked at the top.

Shoes: The bootees of natural leather have flat soles.

Accessories: She carries a mallet for breaking the ground.

42. Girl Reaper. Fourteenth Century

Hair: The girl's hair is loose and hangs down beyond her shoulders.

Headdress: A large-brimmed hat of natural straw is worn.

Garments: The plain three-quarter length dress of dull-green wool has a round neckline, dolman sleeves and a belt at the hips partly hidden by the bloused effect of the dress. It has horizontal stripes of brick-red.

Boots: The girl wears boots of natural leather, buttoned up the front.

Accessories: The girl carries a small sheaf of corn. She wears thick brown leather gauntlet gloves, with a seam down the back.

43. Peasant Woman. Fourteenth Century

Hair: The hair is almost entirely covered by the hood.

Headdress: The hood of natural-coloured wool with a shoulder-piece and *liripipe* is worn casually, with the part intended to cover the head round the neck in front and the *liripipe* hanging down over the right side of the chest.

Garments: The plain red woollen over-dress has long close-fitting sleeves and is a little shorter than the blue under-gown worn beneath it.

Hose: The hose are of grey yarn.

Shoes: The flat-soled black leather shoes come up to the ankle-bones.

Accessories: The woman carries a large farm-worker's fork with horizontal and vertical bars.

44. Townsman or Countryman. About 1340

Hair: This is hidden by the headdress.

Headdress: The man wears a hood of sand-coloured wool with a shoulder-cape. It has been put on carelessly, so that part of the *liripipe* shows under the brim of the round black felt hat, which has an upturned brim and a small ornament on the top.

Garments: The low-waisted *cotehardie* is of brick-red woollen stuff with buttons down the front and a belt and pouch of natural leather at hip-level. The sleeves are long and close-fitting and the skirt ends at the knees.

Hose: The hose are of fawn-coloured woollen stuff.

Footwear: The ankle-boots are of black leather.

Accessories: The man is gardening with a small axe that has an oddly curved blade.

45. Woman with Bow. About 1350

Hair: The hair is in four plaits of which two are visible, pinned up vertically at the sides of the head.

Headdress: The pale-yellow linen hood covers the head and neck and has ties embroidered in green and black on yellow. There are small dagged edges in the front of the hood.

Garments: The under-gown is of coral-red woollen fabric embroidered in an all-over pattern in black, visible at the hem and on the close-fitting inner sleeves. It is fitted to the figure and ends just above the insteps. The outer-gown also clings to the figure and is a little shorter than the under-gown. It is of pale-green wool, bordered at the hem and sleeves in the same design as that on the ties of the hood. The sleeves end just above the elbows and have drooping tabs lined with yellow. This type of over-gown was often lined with fur.

Hose: These are green and can just be seen below the skirt.

Shoes: The flat pointed slippers are of coral-red fabric decorated with gold thread and small gold ornaments.

Accessories: The woman holds a bow from which she has just shot an arrow. A quiver containing arrows is slung diagonally from the right shoulder to the left hip.

46. Baker with Basket and Implement for Lifting Loaves. Mid-Fourteenth Century

Hair: The hair is roughly cut to a short 'bobbed' length.

Headdress: The young man wears a sugar-loaf cap of green felt with an upturned close-fitting brim of yellow. His yellow woollen hood is pushed back on to his shoulders, with the *liripipe* hanging down at the back. The shoulder-cape attached to the hood has dagged edges.

Garments: The low-waisted tunic is of green cloth, with a brown leather belt and pouch. The sleeves are long and plain, showing a little of the yellow under-tunic at the wrists.

Hose: The hose are parti-coloured, one leg being green and the other yellow.

Shoes: The shoes, which come up to the ankle-bone, are of brown leather.

Accessories: The baker carries a basket and an implement for lifting loaves.

47. Housewife or Waiting-Gentlewoman in Gown with Cape Attached. About 1370

Hair: This is unseen beneath the headdress.

Headdress: The arched front of the cap has the shape of the *nebulae* headdress and is made of a wired roll of pale-green gauze, patterned in black. It is attached to a flat-backed cap of black velvet.

Garments: The woman wears a gown of mulberry-pink cloth over an under-gown of green silk of which only the long tight sleeves are seen. The gown is fitted to the figure and ends at the instep. It has a jacket-shaped bodice, buttoned down the front, with facings, a short basque and a flat round collar of green. A long cape matching the pink of the dress is attached to the shoulders in place of sleeves and caught to the side-seams under the arms. In the left inner side of the cape is a pocket into which the woman has put her hand.

Shoes: The flat slippers are of mulberry velvet with criss-cross stitching in green.

48. Lady of the House or Waiting-Gentle-woman with Golden Dish. About 1370

Hair: This is hidden by the headdress.

Headdress: The halo-fronted headdress, made over a stiffened foundation, is of vermilion and dark-green silk, with embroidery in gold thread. A short veil of vermilion silk hangs from it at the back.

Garments: The under-gown of dark-green wool has long close sleeves and is fitted to the figure. The over-dress is of vermilion cloth and, like the under-gown, just clears the floor. Its narrow sideless top also clings to the figure and the seams of the skirt are open from hip to hem, showing a little of the under-gown. Gold stitching ornaments all the edges of the over-gown and gold buttons are sewn down its front to hip-level.

Shoes: The flat slippers are of scarlet leather.

Accessories: A jewelled belt is just visible at the hips. The woman carries a decorated golden dish.

49. Girl with Covered Silver Vessel. about 1370

Hair: The hair is parted in the centre and formed into four plaits, turned up vertically and pinned at the sides of the head.

Garments: The girl wears a *cotehardie*, ending at the instep of yellow woollen fabric. It is fitted to the figure and has black buttons down the front from neck to hem. Two vertical openings on the side-fronts of the skirt are thought to have been used to reach a purse or knife attached to a belt beneath or, when a longer skirt was worn, to facilitate management of the dress. There is a double hem, suggesting that the skirt has been turned up for freedom of movement. The sleeves are made in one with the dress and extend to the elbow, where the ends are covered by long white tippets. The long tight sleeves of the black under-gown of silk, fastened with small silver buttons, continue to the wrists but could be rolled back and the tippets removed for practical work. This dress is sometimes seen in contemporary art on royal ladies, showing that they were glad to be rid of their state robes on occasion.

Shoes: The flat slippers are of black fabric and have pointed toes.

Accessories: The girl carries a covered vessel of silver.

50. Man with Sling. Latter Half of Fourteenth Century

Hair: This can be seen in strands brought forward on the forehead.

Headdress: The yellow woollen hood has a long *liripipe*, black dagged edges, and a fastening down the front starting under the chin and ending at the base of the shoulder-piece.

Garments: The tunic of green cloth is belted at a normal waistline, has a fairly close-fitting body and a slightly flared skirt, and ends rather less than half-way down the thighs. It fastens down the front and has plain close-fitting sleeves.

Hose: These are made like tights. One leg is green and the other yellow, and leather soles take the place of shoes.

Accessories: The belt and the pouch slung from it are of black leather. On the left hip, attached to the belt, is a canvas bag containing stones for the sling carried in the man's right hand. The sling is made of leather and cords, with a container at the bottom where a stone is lodged. Tied to the cords at the point where they pass between the fingers is a small attachment of bone or ivory like a stopper with a flat top, which gives security to the finger-grip. The sling was not much used after the end of the fourteenth century.

CHAPTER THREE
1380–1490

Although feudalism as a rigid social system was virtually at an end, life continued on the large country estates much as it had been for centuries, except that tenants had not only become rent-payers, but were paid for their work in money and in kind.

The nobleman's chief officers were men of good family whose land and houses were derived from their lord, and who were pledged to give him military service. There were marshals of the household, stewards, chamberlains, financial administrators, secretaries, Masters of the Horse and gentlemen-ushers. A steward might act as financial comptroller, and combine this work with his daily duties of riding out with a retinue to inspect the grounds, parkland and pastures to ensure safety and order, and of supervising the giving-out of the day's supply of food, fuel, wine, ale and candles.

The responsibility for the maintenance of rooms, the wardrobe and kitchen departments, the brewery, bakery, dairy, laundry, butchery and cellars, the efficiency of the lower servants and the guardianship of articles of value was in the hands of these officials and those working under them. A chamberlain arranged all the ceremonies connected with the household, and had the special duty of close personal attendance on his lord, of being present at the rituals of his dressing and undressing, and of directing the ushers and grooms of the bedchamber in their work. Where a chaplain was in residence, he might be appointed as financial and legal adviser, land agent, bailiff, secretary and tutor.

Masters of the Horse were responsible for the maintenance of stables, the horses kept for riding and for work, and the guard-dogs on the estate. They and their grooms taught riding to the young people, including squires aspiring to be knights.

Gentleman-ushers (usually lesser noblemen or knights) had the duties of announcing their lord and lady at any place they visited and at all ceremonies, and of lighting their way with torches and candles after dark. They had charge of the valuable tapestries, wall-hangings and bed-coverlets, and might have some duties in the Wardrobe, where the clothes of family and household were kept. They would travel with their lord, sometimes acting as valets and servers of food and drink.

Yeoman-ushers guarded their lord at night and prepared his bed, thrusting daggers into the straw mattress, and rolling on the feather ones laid on the top, to make certain no weapons or assassins were hidden there.

The pages and esquires who waited at table were among the boys of noble birth, usually younger sons, who, according to English custom, were sent away from their homes at seven years of age or thereabouts to be educated in another nobleman's house. In return for their tutoring and training in the accomplishments of a gentleman, they did menial service for their host, rising early from the pallets where they slept at the doors of the knights' rooms and cleaning floors, strewing fresh rushes, lighting fires, hanging the tapestries, and making ready to serve in the Great Hall between seven and eight o'clock. They were taught grammar and rhetoric by the chaplain and were trained in wrestling, running, dancing, hawking and riding, also learning the use of arms from neighbouring knights.

Schools, like those of Eton and Winchester, were founded, and took scholars who paid nothing for their tuition but were charged for their lodgings in the towns or in a tutor's house. Universities at Oxford and Cambridge, and the Inns of Court for legal training, were established.

Girls of the upper classes were also sent away for about seven years to live in the care of a lady of a noble house. They learned the same scholastic subjects as boys and were trained in every department of housewifery, also in fine needlework, languages, music, archery and dancing.

At thirteen or fourteen, a girl was considered marriageable. Long before this age, however, children were nominally married or pledged in a way that was considered binding when they were adolescent. Parents usually arranged the marriages of their children with a view to personal profit, increased family status and ownership of land and titles.

Once married and living in her own home, the lady of a manor-house would supervise and sometimes take part in the preserving of fruit, meat and fish, the care of the poultry, doves and pigeons, the spinning, weaving and making-up of cloth for the dressing of the household, and the ordering in advance from a nearby city of all food that could not be produced on the estate, such as spices, pepper, sugar and Mediterranean wines. She must also be able to help the sick, dispense herbal medicines and tend injuries. It was her duty to wait personally, with the children of the house, on specially honoured guests.

Her gentlewomen worked with her, some of them marrying into the household and remaining as her attendants. Women who did not marry often entered a convent eventually, financial provision being arranged for them in the religious life by their relatives.

The invention of printing, brought to England in 1477 by William Caxton, a merchant and translator with Continental interests who had studied it in an early form in Bruges, brought about the beginning of an immense advance in education and culture. Municipal guilds, merchants and wealthy bishops built and endowed schools. With the vast increase of commercial occupation in England, the literate middle-class was marrying into the minor nobility, creating a new race of landed gentry with more urban connections than had yet been known. This merchant ascendancy, through their guilds, governed the great cities and supplied their kings with money and goods.

London became a rich, prosperous and beautiful city with numerous connections overseas, and like other towns was still pleasantly rural here and there. Large houses of stone and brick were surrounded by gardens, fields and orchards, and their outer boundaries with strips of land for grazing and cultivation. Games, pageants, plays, hunting, contests in wrestling, running and archery on which wagers were laid were the recreations from hard-driving commerce, the cottage industries of spinning and weaving, and the arduous labour of the fields.

COSTUME OF THE PERIOD: 1380–1490

Hair—Men: Hair could be cut to a 'bobbed' length throughout this period. The fashion of cutting the hair in a pudding-basin shape, shaved up to ear-level at the back, returned from about 1413 to mid-century, and was sometimes so short that it was invisible when a hat was worn. In many instances long hair to the shoulders was worn from about 1460.

Hair—Women: Women's hair was partly seen under the reticulated headdress when this was unlined, but was almost entirely hidden by the headdress for the remainder of the period.

Headdress—Men: The main items of headdress from the latter part of the fourteenth century until the middle of the fifteenth were the *chaperon* and the byecocket. The latter had a tall cone-shaped crown, upright or leaning backward, and a brim turned up at the back with a long peak in front. A form of turban was worn between 1440 and 1460. Hats and caps in varied shapes, some very eccentric, were worn throughout, including a soft-crowned cap with a peak falling to one side, or two peaks falling on opposite sides and a close-fitting upturned brim, a hat with a wide brim rolled upward at the sides, a head-fitting cap turned up at the back with a short brim in front, and tall-crowned caps from mid-century onwards.

Headdress—Women: The small turban-shaped headdress and the flat, horizontal type worn with the hair coiled over the ears or at the temples, both worn with a short veil at the back, gave place at the beginning of the fifteenth century to a wider, more elaborate fashion, with the veil in some cases hanging at the sides as well as at the back. This developed a dip in the centre, and the ends of the headdress were gradually brought upward and closer together, forming first the heart-shaped and then the forked headdress. Veils decorated these rolls and frameworks. The butterfly headdress, a contrivance of layers of gauze on a wire frame, was another fashion starting about the same time, lasting in various shapes until 1480. Turbans were worn between 1440 and 1460, and some eccentric variations of this were seen. The hennin, a tall cone-shaped structure pointed at the top, but sometimes truncated to a flat-topped shape, appeared about 1430 and was worn with different types of veil until 1480. A band of velvet or satin added to the hennin was in most cases laid across the front of the head. Many different hoods, veils and caps were worn for domestic and manual labour and by country-dwellers.

Garments—Men: The *houppeland* was the most important garment from about 1380 until 1460. Its long flowing lines continued, but other versions of it ended at knee-, ankle- or calf-level. With shorter skirts bag-sleeves, generally with an opening for the arm at the elbow as well as at the wrist, took the place of the long wide sleeves. Dagged edges to sleeves and skirts were in fashion until mid-century.

Normal and low waistlines were worn with the *houppeland*. The very short tunic abandoned the double-level waistline for a normal one after the first decade. A tunic with a full knee-length skirt arranged in stitched padded pleats had a low or normal waistline. The cassock, a longer but similar garment, could end below the knee, or at calf- or ankle-level. It often had a front slit or side-slits in the skirt of moderate width all the way down, bag-sleeves or sleeves wrinkling over the arms and a low or normal waistline. It was in fashion from the first decade to the middle of the century. At this time a type of closed gown was introduced, with similar sleeves and padded pleats running down the centre from the shoulders, converging at the waist or from the waist only, and descending to the hem. By 1460 a short tunic with puff-shouldered over-sleeves was in fashion, also a gown worn closed or open, belted or loose, with sleeves of the same type or bag-sleeves that sometimes hung from the shoulders. This gown could be open from armpit to hem at the sides, or waist to hem in front, and was worn over the tunic. A full loose tunic ended at the hips and was unbelted. Another version of it was worn as a sleeveless outer garment and ended at the calf. The short forms of tunic and those ending at the knee or a little above, also the short *houppeland*, were worn by artisans, labourers and tradesmen in this period.

Garments—Women: The *houppeland* with long, wide sleeves worn towards the end of the fourteenth century continued into the fifteenth and became the most important of women's fashions. The high closed collar could be worn open, and a flat, round turned-down collar fastening at the base of the throat came in. In the 1420s the high waistline was lowered a little to a broad belt, and a wide collar just covered the shoulders and came down to a point where it met the belt. It was usually of fur or velvet. The bosom of the dress was filled in by the top of the undergown, the chemise, or added folds of lawn or gauze. Bag-sleeves or moderately wide sleeves wrinkled over the arms could be worn. After 1460 long, narrow sleeves with cuffs turned back took the place of the former sleeves. A form of the *houppeland* was made just touching the ground, with less voluminous skirts than usual for practical wear, but the garment did not lend itself readily to this use, and the ordinary *houppeland* was difficult to pin up.

The *cotehardie* persisted into the first quarter of the fifteenth century and remained in a shortened form for working women until a later date. The open-sided gown was retained only as a ceremonial dress for royalty or nobility.

The 'round' dress was useful for active pursuits. It appeared about 1460 and had a skirt clearing the ground, a fitted bodice and long close-fitting sleeves.

Hose—Men: Long hose made as a complete garment were worn with leather soles attached or with shoes or boots.

Hose—Women: Women's hose, as in the preceding century, are thought to have been gartered at the knee.

Footwear—Men: The long pointed toes made with the *pouleynes* of the late fourteenth century diminished at the beginning of the fifteenth, but increased again, reaching their greatest length about 1460 and then growing less again until the broad-toed shoes of the new fashion were introuced about 1485. Bootees, boots ending below the knee and thigh-boots, both laced on the inside of the leg, were made with the fashionable toes or with more normal ones for active pursuits. Mules with flat soles and normal toes were worn. Footwear worn by men engaged in practical work was moderately pointed or of normal shape. The wooden clog or *galoche* was long and pointed.

Footwear—Women: Women's shoes were less exaggeratedly pointed than those of men.

Materials, Colour and Ornament: This period was one of great splendour for the well-to-do. For those wearing more practical dress woollen homespun, cloth of varying weights, fustian velvet, cotton, linen and lawn were used. Colours for these workaday clothes were brown, blue, slate-colour, orange, purple, scarlet, crimson, green, yellow, saffron, amber, russet, red-brown, white and black. Servants and attendants might wear identical parti-coloured clothes.

51. Gentleman-Servitor, Administrator in a Nobleman's House. Late Fourteenth Century

Hair: The hair is curled and cut in a short 'bobbed' fashion.

Headdress: The hat of sherry-brown velvet has a round, head-fitting crown and a brim that is turned up at the back and has a long peak in front. A brilliant green feather is attached to the brim at the back. The hat is a forerunner of the *byecocket*.

Garments: The long close-fitting gown is of dark amber velvet, with decoration to the shoulder-cape in gold and green. It has gold buttons down the front to hip-level. The hood is folded on the shoulders and its gilt buttons and brilliant green lining are seen at the front of the neck. The sleeves are close-fitting and have goblet cuffs.

Shoes: The pointed shoes are of sherry-brown velvet, decorated in gold.

Accessories: The man holds a stylus (a pen for writing on wax) in the right hand and hinged ivory tablets, with a writing-surface of wax, in the left.

52. Gentleman-Servitor Supervising Work for his Master. Closing Years of Fourteenth Century

Hair: The hair is curled and cut in a 'bobbed' shape.

Headdress: The *chaperon* is of cherry-red velvet, with dagged edges pointing forward over the forehead and a close-fitting upturned brim.

Garments: The man is wearing a short, close-fitting, high-necked tunic of black velvet with long close sleeves to the wrists. Over it is a three-quarter length gown of ivory cloth lined with cherry-red silk. It has dagged edges and deep wide sleeves with a comparatively small hand-opening, which shows the red lining as the dagged edges fall back. The gown is made like a tabard, the front hanging loose and the back caught in at hip-level by the jewelled belt of the tunic.

Hose: The left leg of the hose is cherry-coloured and is decorated with a jewelled garter below the knee. The right leg is black. Leather soles are attached.

Accessories: The man has a small dagger slung on a cord and hanging at the back of his shoulders.

53. Page in Parti-Coloured Dress. End of Four-teenth, Beginning of Fifteenth Centuries

Hair: The hair is cut in a 'bobbed' shape and curves forward on the cheeks.

Headdress: The circular head-fitting cap is in felt, cloth or velvet, and is parti-coloured in black, white and pale green.

Garments: The short close-fitting doublet has a rounded neckline at the base of the throat and long, close-fitting sleeves. It has a seam defining the natural waistline now coming back into fashion, but a belt ornamented in black and green is worn additionally at hip-level. The garment is parti-coloured like the cap.

Hose: The long hose, made like tights, are in the same parti-colours as the cap and doublet. They have leather soles.

Accessories: The page carries his master's helmet and lance, with banner attached.

54. Serving-Woman. Early Fifteenth Century

Hair: This is hidden by the headdress.

Headdress: The white linen hood has a neckpiece and a long strip at the back. This can be brought over the shoulder to hand or wipe dishes.

Garments: The *cotehardie* of blue wool is fitted to the figure and has plain close-fitting sleeves and a full skirt just clearing the ground. Its black belt is worn low, attached to the dress all round, as it serves no purpose except to hold the purse.

Shoes: The flat slippers are of black leather or fabric.

Accessories: The purse is of black fabric. The woman carries a glass bowl containing a whole pickled fish in liquid.

55. Waiting-Gentlewoman carrying her Lady's Hat. Early Fifteenth Century

Hair: This is unseen beneath the headdress.

Headdress: The woman wears a turban of pink silk in two shades, one much darker than the other, on a stiffened foundation.

Garments: The dress is in the lighter pink with the border at the neck, the ends of the short outer sleeves, the belt, and the hem in the darker shade. The under-gown, of which the high neck and the long close sleeves can be seen, is of parchment-coloured silk. Tucks or pleats descend from the square neckline of the outer gown and are released at hip-level above the belt.

Hose: These are of parchment-colour.

Shoes: The sandals are of scarlet leather with thick soles slightly raised at the back.

Accessories: The waiting-woman carries her lady's hat of white velvet, decorated with leaves of pearl-coloured satin edged with pearls.

56. Shepherdess. Early Fifteenth Century

Hair: The hair is covered by the headdress.

Headdress: A plain rectangle of white cotton is worn, fastened by two of its corners at the back of the head.

Garments: The over-dress of shabby light-blue wool fits the figure closely and has a laced bodice and sleeves ending raggedly below the shoulders. The long sleeves and part of the skirt of the white cotton chemise are seen.

Shoes: The feet are bare.

Accessories: The girl carries a sheep-crook.

57. Elderly Nurse and Child. Early Fifteenth Century

Hair: The nurse's hair is hidden by her headdress. The child's hair is cut fairly short.

Headdress: The nurse wears a white linen hood with a *liripipe* brought forward over the forehead and a shoulder-cape.

Garments: Her *cotehardie* is of grey woollen stuff with a fitted bodice, close-fitting sleeves, long white tippets from the elbows and a full gored skirt just clearing the floor. A black swathed girdle with a purse attached is worn at hip-level. The child wears a white gown with a square-cut neckline and long sleeves.

Shoes: The nurse's flat slippers are of black fabric and the child's of scarlet silk.

Accessories: The child carries a ball.

58. Woman with Water-Sprinkler. About 1410

Hair: A little of the hair can be seen under the hat.

Headdress: The hat is of deep-blue felt with ornament of gold thread.

Garments: The gown of thin pale-blue wool is a *cotehardie*, but has large wide sleeves with dagged edges. It has a round neckline fitting the base of the neck, and the body of it clings to the figure. The skirt is less flowing than that of the usual *cotehardie* and gives greater freedom of movement. The applied or embroidered motifs decorating it are in deep blue and gold.

Shoes: The soft flat slippers are of biscuit-coloured kid.

Accessories: The woman is sprinkling a pot of flowers with water from a container that has holes in the base. The sprinkler is probably made of metal and enamel work in varied colours and presumably contains some mechanism at the top that releases the water on pressure or rotation.

59. Farm-Labourer. Fifteenth Century

Hair: This is seen only in strands over the forehead.

Headdress: The hood and shoulder-piece (with dagged edges) are of dark-green woollen stuff. A hat of soft rust-coloured material is turned back from the face and draped in a short *liripipe* on the left side.

Garments: The plain tunic is of dark copper-coloured woollen fabric and the cloak, which fastens at the throat and is thrown back over the right shoulder, is of rust-red wool. It is fastened down to the leather belt by two leather straps.

Hose: The leggings of coarse brown yarn are worn over hose of green cloth.

Shoes: Stout shoes of brown leather are worn.

Accessories: The labourer carries a kind of scythe. A bag made of rectangles of sacking to hold tools or other belongings is slung on one side of his belt and a leather pouch on the other.

60. Man Treading Grapes. French 1440s

Hair: This has been partly shaved and is not visible under the hat.

Headdress: The hat is a *chaperon* of black woollen stuff.

Garments: The man wears white under-drawers and an under-doublet of green glazed cotton, with long close-fitting sleeves and lacing down the front.

Footwear: His legs and feet are bare.

Accessories: He is treading grapes in a large wooden tub.

61. Man with Flail. Mid-Fifteenth Century

Hair : The hair is trimmed to a 'bobbed' length.

Headdress : The hat is of straw, with its round brim turned up at both sides.

Garments : The plain tunic is of pinkish brick-red woollen stuff and ends at the knees. It has plain three-quarter length sleeves.

Hose : The coarse woollen hose are rolled and gartered below the knee over inner hose.

Footwear : Stout leather bootees are worn.

Accessories : The man is wielding a flail. He wears a leather sheath containing a knife slung from his belt.

62. Messenger. Mid-Fifteenth Century

Hair : The hair is cut in a 'bobbed' shape.

Headdress : The large hat has a head-fitting flat-topped crown (unseen) and a wide brim turned up all round giving a turban-shaped effect. It is made up of swathes of silk in black, carnation-red and pink draped on a stiffened linen or canvas foundation.

Garments : The doublet has a close-fitting high collar, a skirt ending above the knees, and 'mahoytered' shoulders to the sleeves, which are close-fitting in the lower part. The messenger is in the service of a noble house and wears his master's coat-of-arms as a badge on his left breast. His clothes are in his master's colours of black, pink and carnation-red. The belt and pouch are of white leather.

Hose : The hose are parti-coloured to match the doublet.

Footwear : The ankle-boots are of white leather.

Accessories : The messenger carries a letter for delivery.

63. Attorney, Clerk or Architect. About 1450

Hair: The hair is straight and is cut short all round to a level above the ears, leaving a shaven part at the back of the head.

Headdress: A round brimless hat of beaver felt, with a long bright-green scarf attached, is carried on the shoulder.

Garments: The high collar and sleeves of the under-tunic of amber-coloured woollen stuff are partly seen at the neck and wrists. The gown is of tan-orange woollen fabric and has a narrow edging of brown fur at the neck, where there is a vertical opening to admit the head, and at the wrists and hem. It is narrower in cut than the *houppeland* and was known as a cassock. It fastens down the front and ends just above the shoes. A leather belt is worn at hip-level. The sleeves are plain and of the same width all the way down.

Hose: These are of a neutral light-brown colour.

Shoes: The shoes, of brown leather, have pointed but not elongated toes. Pointed shapes cover the insteps and the backs of the ankles.

Accessories: The man carries a quill pen and has a 'penner' (a case for quills) and inkwell of leather and metal slung at his belt.

64. Judge. About 1450

Hair: This is of 'bobbed' length and can be seen below the back of his coif and over his forehead.

Headdress: A white linen coif is worn.

Garments: The judge wears a 'cassock' or robe of heavy scarlet silk, just clearing the ground. The sleeves are of moderate width, sewn into bands and edged with white fur at the wrists. Part of a red shoulder-cape, also edged with white fur, can be seen. The semicircular cloak is of scarlet cloth lined with white fur, and is fastened on the right shoulder. It has a hood collar, thrown back and turned down in front to show the fur lining. At this time legal dress was only beginning to be stabilised and many judges had taken to wearing scarlet.

Footwear: The slippers are of scarlet leather.

Accessories: The judge is holding an open book.

65. Tailor. Mid-Fifteenth Century

Hair: The hair has been shaved all round the head, up to the level of the ears at the back and sides, leaving a small circular shape of straight hair on the top of the head (unseen).

Headdress: The hat of green felt, with a large, rigid, up-turned brim, has an edging of ruched gold binding.

Garments: The calf-length under-tunic is of black woollen stuff and has short sleeves ending below the shoulders, with long close-fitting sleeves as well. The over-tunic of scarlet wool is a little shorter in the skirt and has castellated dagged edges at the hem and the ends of the short sleeves. The flowing sleeves of scarlet woollen fabric lined with green are attached to the short sleeves of the under-tunic.

Hose: The hose have flat leather soles attached to serve instead of shoes. One leg is green and the other scarlet.

Accessories: A purse of white velvet shaped like a flower is attached to the gilt leather belt. The tailor holds a pair of scissors and a measuring-stick.

66. Woman in *Houppeland* with Skirts Pinned up. 1440–50

Hair: This is hidden by the headdress.

Headdress: The *bicorne* headdress is mounted on a jewelled net which covers the hair. The ivory silk veil laid over the framework is knotted at the base of the skull on the left-hand side and has an end hanging free on the right.

Garments: The gown is an example of the unsuitably rich clothes worn during the Renaissance for hunting or fishing. It is a *houppeland* of turquoise-blue grosgrain with dark-rose, deep-blue, and silver ornament. The neckline is wide, with ivory silk gauze filling it in on the shoulders and a goffered frill across the bosom. The under-gown, which can be seen at the hem, is of rose-coloured silk with a border to the skirt of four rows of silver edging. The long close sleeves of this are visible. Draped extra sleeves of ivory silk are attached to the short outer sleeves, which are turned up with silver.

Shoes: Long pointed flat-soled shoes of rose-coloured fabric with criss-cross silver ornament are worn.

Jewellery and Accessories: The woman wears a necklace of silver and turquoise. She carries a fishing-rod in order to join an angling party which will help to provide food for the household.

67. Woman Going to Market. About 1460

Hair: This is unseen beneath the hood.

Headdress: The back of the unbleached linen hood is seen, with two *liripipes* hanging down, one with its end tucked into the girdle. The hood comes to a point at each side of the head.

Garments: The blue-grey woollen dress, seen from the back, is pulled up and pouched over a girdle (unseen) to make it shorter. The sleeves are full, diminishing a little towards the wrists.

Accessories: The woman carries a basket containing produce for the market on each arm and another on her head.

68. Gentleman-Servitor. About 1460

Hair: The hair is 'bobbed' and slightly curled, covering the ears.

Headdress: The young man wears a *byecocket* of lime-green and red-purple silk sewn in elongated triangular segments on to a stiffened foundation. The triangles are joined in a knot at the top, with short streamers of the silk forming a tassel. The brim is green on the upper side and purple on the lower. The edge is piped in a brilliant red shot with silver, which also edges the segments and forms part of the tassel.

Garments: The long close-fitting sleeves of a dark-purple under-doublet are seen below the sleeves of the lime-green doublet. These have raised shoulders, the right sleeve being really a small puffed shoulder-cape and the left draped to meet the waist of the doublet. The bodice has two rows of converging pleats from shoulder to hem, with additional pleats in the centre. The belted waist slopes downwards to the short skirts. The garment is piped in the bright red and silver at the neck, sleeve edges, belt and hem.

Hose: One leg of the leather-soled hose is lime-green and the other purple.

Accessories: The man carries a sword, unsheathed, with the scabbard worn at his hip.

69. London Merchant. About 1460

Hair: The hair is curled, turning inward at the ends, and parted in the centre. It is long enough to cover the ears. The beard and moustache are neatly trimmed.

Garments: The merchant wears a gown of coral-red cloth ending at the insteps, embroidered with motifs in gold thread. Its loose-fitting sleeves are of the same width throughout. The sleeves of a brown silk under-gown are seen at the wrists. The cloak of pinkish-red cloth, lighter in colour than the gown, is lined with fur and turned back over the left shoulder. It has a high collar and fastens with buttons on the right shoulder.

Shoes: The flat-soled shoes of brown velvet follow the shape of the foot.

Accessories: The merchant holds a pair of scales and a small bag containing money.

70. Elderly Female Beggar. Fifteenth Century

Hair: This hardly shows beneath the headdress.

Headdress: A length of dirty unbleached linen is pinned at the top of the head, brought round under the chin, over the head, and allowed to hang down on the left side.

Garments: The long gown of indeterminate neutral colour trails on the ground as the woman walks but is raised over the left knee to show her swollen and bandaged leg. The plain long sleeves show the ends of the sleeves of the shabby dark-grey under-gown.

Shoes: Old shoes of buff leather are worn.

Accessories: The woman has a basket strapped to her back by a strap across her chest which is kept in place by metal fasteners attached to her dress. A sack is hung over the basket. She holds a walking-stick in her left hand and a crutch under her right arm.

71. Waterman in Fishing-Boat. 1460–70

Hair: The hair is cut in a fairly short 'bobbed' shape, in this instance blown back by the wind.

Garments: The boatman wears a tunic ending at mid-thigh and belted at the waist. It is one often seen in fifteenth-century art and has moderately full sleeves tapering from the middle of the forearm to the wrist. The tunic is of woollen stuff in a dull darkish pink and the short cloak matches it.

Hose: The hose, made like tights, match the tunic and cloak.

Shoes: The shoes are not seen, but could be of black buck-skin, slightly pointed, following the shape of the foot and coming up in points over the insteps and the heels.

Accessories: The man is standing in the sharp, uprising prow of his small fishing-boat, bringing it round by means of a pole with a cross-bar for holding it.

72. Waiting-Gentlewoman with Rosary. 1460–80

Hair: This is hidden by the headdress.

Headdress: The tall 'butterfly'-type headdress is of fine white gauze draped on a wire frame which is attached to a truncated hennin in violet, crimson and silver.

Garments: The woman wears the gown known as a round dress of heavy grey-violet satin-surfaced stuff. It is slightly high-waisted and the skirt, which has a border of grey fur, touches the ground. A deep collar of the fur encircles the back of the neck and comes down over the bosom, the two sides meeting at the waist. The open bodice is filled in with folds of white silk gauze. The sleeves are long and close-fitting, with fur cuffs. The belt is of silvered leather ornamented in violet and crimson.

Hose: Flat slippers of grey fabric are worn.

Accessories: The woman wears a necklace of amethyst and crystal fitting the neck closely. She is holding a rosary.

73. Pharmacist's Assistant. About 1470

Hair: The hair is fairly long and is ragged and unkempt.

Headdress: A shabby version of a byecocket in green felt is worn.

Garments: The sleeves of the rust-coloured woollen tunic are rolled up, also those of the white shirt, whose collar can be partly seen.

Hose: The hose are of light-brown wool.

Shoes: Bootees of brown buckskin are worn, with clumsy wooden and leather pattens over them.

Accessories: The youth wears a light-brown leather belt to which are attached a small bottle, a sheathed knife, a purse, a penner containing a quill pen and an inkwell. He is pounding or stirring with a long stick some substance in a large stoneware jar.

74. Musician with Monkey (Italian Style). Closing Years of Fifteenth Century

Hair: The hair is worn in a fringe on the forehead and hangs in curls to the shoulders.

Headdress: The tall, brimless hat of shabby bright-pink plush has a flat top.

Garments: The yellow shirt shows at openings in the front and at the base of the doublet, and at openings in the shoulders and sleeves. These are tied by points. The doublet of dark-maroon cloth ends at the waist. Its open front is laced across the front of the shirt.

Hose: The yellow hose are made like tights, but expose the toes and heels, as they are meant to be worn with shoes, which the man lacks. The codpiece is tied with points.

Accessories: He is playing a form of trumpet. A monkey dressed in a tunic and breeches sits on his shoulder.

75. Monastic Habit. Renaissance Onwards

Hair: The hair is tonsured.

Garments: The habit of brown sackcloth fits loosely, and part of its skirt is pulled up over the rope girdle to give freedom of movement. The girdle has three knots in it to symbolise the vows of poverty, chastity and obedience.

Footwear: Brown leather sandals are worn over bare feet.

Accessories: The book is a breviary or other religious work.

CHAPTER FOUR
1490–1590

England in 1485 was an agricultural country. Its towns were small and its population less than one-tenth of what it is today. The year 1485 marked the end of thirty years of civil war known as the Wars of the Roses, and Henry VII, the first of the Tudor rulers, became king. He made his position more secure by disbanding the armed retainers who had been in the pay of noblemen. Large numbers of these men became outlaws and joined robber bands already living in uncleared forest land. The standing army did not yet exist and the use of mercenaries could not now be supplemented by the private armies of the noblemen. During the Hundred Years War, which ended in 1453, however, a compulsory militia system for home defence had been set up which, by the reign of Elizabeth I, could put a body of highly trained men in the field at short notice. Mercenaries augmented any military force. The arquebus and pike were fast replacing the longbow, which, however, remained a useful weapon. The development of cannon meant that castles, as places of defence and refuge, were vulnerable.

Henry VIII created the Royal Navy, broke with the Church of Rome, and became Supreme Head of the English Church. He dissolved the monasteries, disposing of their lands and revenues as he pleased. Large numbers of monastery servants were thrown out of work. Some of them were absorbed into the households of the new landed gentry who bought monastic lands from the king. Other less employable dependants of the monasteries joined a workless vagrant class often referred to as 'sturdy beggars' who terrorised isolated villages and homes. Their ranks were swollen by men ousted from agricultural employment by the enclosure of arable land turned into pasture to graze sheep. The few shepherds required for flocks of sheep replaced the larger numbers who had been required to till the land. The wool obtained from the sheep was needed for the important English wool and cloth trade. A rise in prices and in the cost of living added to the difficulties.

The problems of unemployment continued into Elizabeth's reign, and efforts were made to deal with them. A Vagrancy Act passed in 1549 dealt severely with beggars; they were whipped or branded and if caught again were made slaves. This law was soon repealed, and measures were slowly evolved to distinguish the rogue from the genuine unemployed man. The first general Poor Law passed in 1601 classified the unemployed into the able-bodied, the infirm and aged, and the sturdy rogues—the first to be 'set to work', the second to be cared for, and the third to be disciplined.

The movement westward from Constantinople of treasure and scholarship which followed the fall of that city to the Turks in 1453 resulted in the stimulation of many branches of thought and culture. In Italy, the first country to receive and engender the full burgeoning of the Renaissance, magnificent paintings and sculpture, furnishings of great luxury and beauty, goldsmiths' work in precious stones and metals and an Oriental-classical style of architecture, were the results of the knowledge and artistry salvaged from the wreck of the once powerful Eastern Empire.

This was the time of the great Italian painters and sculptors. Leonardo da Vinci, Michelangelo, Raphael and many others had as their patrons such wealthy and powerful trading families as the Medici in Florence, whose most famous member was known as Lorenzo the Magnificent. Another Florentine, Niccolo Machiavelli, put forward in his book *The Prince* the theory that the great test of statesmanship was success and that scruples and morals were out of place in its pursuit.

In the field of science and invention, the steering of ships was improved by the use of lateen sails and the navigation of river-locks by the swing gates designed by Leonardo da Vinci to replace the guillotine type. A crane with a jib-arm could now lift weighty objects clear of the side of a building; a cranked winch supplied another means of raising them. The rolling mill that could press gold, silver and copper to mint coins, a dredger for cleaning harbours, estuaries and rivers, the lead pencil and the spanner all appeared. Clear glass was put in the larger latticed windows of houses now being built and Venetian-style drinking glasses began to replace pewter drinking vessels.

University studies were revived as scholars and philosophers found ready listeners in many European countries. In due course the new flowering of the intellect and imagination created an age rich in drama, literature and poetry.

Shakespeare, Marlowe, Ben Jonson and Francis Bacon were contemporaries in England of Cervantes and Lope de Vega in Spain and of Ronsard and Montaigne in France. The universal spirit of restlessness and enquiry extended to the voyages of exploration that brought back to Europe news of discoveries in lands till then unknown.

COSTUME OF THE PERIOD: 1490–1590

Hair—Men: Hair was fairly long at first with a fringe or centre-parting, and turned in at the ends. Short hair appeared about 1515–20, and was established by 1530, usually brought forward without a parting. It could be worn *en brosse* from 1570, and from 1580 brushed back in an arc or to one side, or in short curls all over; it was now a little longer at the back. Men could be clean-shaven or have fringe beards with narrow moustaches meeting them. There were shaped moustaches with or without short trimmed beards by 1540. A longer pointed beard was in fashion from 1560 and from 1570 the moustache could point upwards at the ends. Older men could wear forked, spade-shaped or goatee beards.

Hair—Women: Hair was parted in the centre, showing only a little in front at first. It could hang loose under the veil at the back or be bound to the head by ribbons and pins. After 1525 it was worn in a flat chignon or two crossed swathes at the back. After 1540 more hair showed at the temples and was often curled or crimped. Frames or pads were used to widen the coiffure. After 1570 hair was usually taken back in an arc over a pad, often with a dip in the centre.

Headdress—Men: Tall, brimless or soft low-crowned caps were worn in the 1480s and '90s; segmented, buttoned-back caps throughout the period for artisans, citizens and professional men; larger-brimmed versions until approximately 1530; a pill-box shape, tilted over a caul, from 1520 until mid-century; a stiffened brimless cap, moulded to have four corners, worn chiefly by scholars and statesmen throughout, and from mid-century the 'flat' cap with a soft, low crown and narrow brim, and a higher crown after 1550. The *copotain*, with a tall crown and narrow undulating brim, was worn from this time onwards. The coif, in black or white, was worn by scholars, statesmen and elderly men.

Headdress—Women: The hood with lappets at sides and back of the 1480s became the gabled headdress which lasted into the 1540s. A plain linen hood with a downward curve in front and sides curving forward developed into a headdress with a pendent veil, and later into the Marie Stuart cap of the 1570s onwards.

The French hood worn throughout had a horseshoe shape. Its veil, stiffened and turned forward, created the *bongrâce* headdress. Caps of lawn and linen in varied shapes, set back on the head, were worn throughout. Jewelled nets and cauls, also small cylindrical caps called *escoffions*, were in fashion from the 1550s to '70s. A large hood covering headdress and ruff was in fashion from 1580. Women copied men's hats in the 1570s.

Garments—Men: Skirtless doublets with slashed sleeves and open, laced-together fronts showing the shirt were worn from the 1480s with hose forming complete tights. Tunics ending just above or below the knees were worn until about 1510. 'Bases' or kilt-like skirts made up of padded pleats were in vogue until 1520. They were sometimes attached to a sleeveless bodice, and a skirtless, full-sleeved doublet was worn with them. They were fashionable among civilian gentry, upper servants and gentlemen-at-arms.

The doublet was a body-fitting garment with a short basque from about 1520. From about 1575 to 1590 the peascod-belly was fashionable for gentlemen and upper servants. Slashed and paned doublet-fronts and sleeves were usual. Shoulder-rolls and 'wings' were worn until the 1580s, when the full 'trunk' sleeves came in. The turned-back cuff appeared in place of the hand-ruff about 1580. The doublet was at first collarless. By the 1530s a collar-band had appeared, with a narrow frill which became the small ruff. The large ruff, worn by genty, appeared about 1580, also the 'falling-band'.

Labourers wore a loose, belted tunic which almost hid the breeches. Close-fitting breeches were worn over hose or, in the early years, attached to them. By 1525 breeches could be fuller and sewn into a band well above the knee. They formed a separate garment and became padded and paned 'round-hose' by the 1550s. 'Venetians' were worn from 1570.

From the 1520s the short-sleeved or sleeveless jerkin was often worn over the doublet. It could have a deep skirt or a basque until the 1560s, but after that date a basque only. Short cloaks shaped as three-quarters of a circle were worn from the 1550s to '80s; longer ones at the end of the epoch.

Long and short outer gowns, with wide long revers and hanging sleeves, were worn all through the period until the 1570s.

Garments—Women: Bodice and kirtle comprised the new fashion in the 1480s. Long sleeves showed below the wide turned-back over-sleeves. A partlet or chemise-frill was visible within the usually square neckline of the over-dress. Skirts had trains and the boned bodices rounded waistlines. Some gowns resembling the *cotehardie* persisted. By the 1530s the pyramidal Spanish farthingale had given a rigid appearance to the skirt, but petticoats were more usual for practical work. Most dresses were open in front from waist to hem, showing the kirtle. Many skirts were circular. A high collar topped by a small ruff was worn.

By mid-century the waistline was pointed, and some dresses were closed in front. Close-fitting sleeves with 'mahoytered' shoulders and hand-ruffs were in fashion. From 1580 'trunk' sleeves with hanging sleeves and larger ruffs were worn. The French 'roll' farthingale was an innovation. The stomacher created a deeper point to the bodice. The 'wheel' farthingale was worn by 1590. The loose open gown became an outer garment about 1550. Others were long mantles and square wraps folded into a triangle.

Stockings—Men: These were known early in the period, but complete tights were contemporaneous. 'Canions' were worn from the 1580s. Stockings could be rolled over the knees with these or with 'Venetians'. Working men wore hose of coarse yarn, wool, linen, or cloth cut on the cross.

Stockings—Women: Women's stockings were gartered at the knee. They were of fine knitted material or of stuff cut on the cross and seamed.

Footwear—Men: Broad-toed mules and shoes were worn until the 1530s. After this shoes followed the shape of the foot, had fairly high vamps and were decorated with cuts and slashes. Thigh-boots of soft wrinkled leather with wide toes were worn at first. From the 1530s they were shaped to the leg. Labourers wore leggings and stout short boots.

Footwear—Women: Women's shoes were like those of men.

Materials, Colour and Ornament: Cloth, plush, mohair, fustian velvet, frieze and other woollens with tufts or knots as embellishment, linen and some cotton were available for workaday dress. Ornament included metal rings, beads, buttons and braid sewn on, also tabbed edging, slashing, paning and pinking. Colours were brown, blue, grey, dun-colour, purple, russet and black, with bright shades of red, yellow, amber, terra-cotta and orange for simply dressed people.

Those wearing more elaborate garments would have the finest materials in all fashionable colours with rich decoration.

76. Gentleman-Servitor. About 1490

Hair: The hair is cropped short.

Headdress: The tall soft-crowned brimless cap is of black velvet. It is worn tilted over the brow.

Garments: Part of the white shirt is seen at the neck and at the waist. The waist-length under-doublet is of violet and silver shot silk. Only the back of the shoulders and part of the right sleeve are seen. The over-doublet is of black velvet. It ends at the waist and has large open cape sleeves bordered with grey fur, which also edges the wide oval neckline.

Hose: The hose, made as a complete garment from the waist down, with leather soles attached in place of shoes, are parti-coloured in black and violet.

Accessories: The man is holding a large sheathed sword, probably for use in some ceremony.

77. Italian Serving-Maid or Nurse with Baby. About 1490

Hair: This is parted in the centre and is seen only in front.

Headdress: The white linen veil is laid over the head and fastened at the back of the neck. The remainder is brought up from the back and the ends spread over the brow and arranged to frame the face.

Garments: The dress of dark-blue linen has a high waist and long sleeves, slightly full at the elbow. The belt is of black velvet. A long narrow white apron is worn. The baby is wrapped in white swaddling-clothes.

Shoes: The soft flat slippers are of scarlet leather.

78. Maid-Servant or Country-Dweller. 1485–1500

Hair: The hair is parted in the centre, unseen beneath the cap.

Headdress: The hood is made of two rectangles of brown cloth seamed together on two adjoining sides to form a point at the back, with the other two left open to show the face. A slit is made on each side to allow room for the shoulders. The front is turned back to frame the face.

Garments: The gown is of claret-coloured cloth. It has a bodice fitted to the figure and a fairly high square neckline showing a white partlet beneath. The full skirt is turned up and draped over the hips, showing part of a moss-green kirtle.

Shoes: The flat-soled shoes of brown buckskin or fabric have very broad toes.

Accessories: The girl carries a short-handled skillet.

79. Armed Servant of an Italian Nobleman. About 1490

Hair: The hair is short and only a little of it can be seen beneath the cap.

Headdress: A round cap of black felt is worn.

Garments: The scarlet doublet has a small standing collar of black velvet, open in front to show the white collar-band of the shirt. Its basque is short and the narrow belt points downward from the back to the front. The upper sleeve is very short. The matching lower sleeves are tied in by points above the elbow. The seam has openings from elbow to wrist, showing the shirt-sleeve.

Hose: The hose are made as a garment reaching the waist and are parti-coloured in black and green. The straps across the buttocks help to keep the hose in place.

Shoes: The shoes are of black buckskin.

Accessories: The servant wears a sword in its scabbard at his left hip.

80. Serving-Man. About 1500

Hair: The hair is long, ending just below the shoulders, and is parted (unseen) in the centre.

Headdress: The black velvet cap has a close-fitting segmented brim, turned up all round. A small curving feather is attached on the right side of the front, inside the brim.

Garments: The neckline and a little of one close-fitting sleeve belonging to a green under-tunic can just be seen. The over-tunic of crimson cloth has a rounded neckline and buttons down the front. It fits loosely at the slightly low waist and has a fairly full skirt ending just below the knees. The long loose over-sleeves are moderately full.

Hose: The hose are green.

Shoes: The green velvet shoes have very broad toes and a strap across the instep.

Accessories: The man is carrying two covered silver serving-dishes, one above the other.

81. Lady of the House. With Purse and Keys. About 1485–1500

Hair: This is parted in the centre and only a little of it is seen over the brow.

Headdress: A cap made up of triangular segments of silk in black, yellow and turquoise-blue on a stiffened foundation is set on the back of the head. It has a small round ornament where the segments join at the top of the cap. In front is a band of black velvet, also stiffened, whose ends stand out at the back beyond the shoulder-blades.

Garments: The gown of yellow cloth is shaped to the body and has a round untrimmed neckline. The sleeves are plain and end at the elbows, an unusual feature showing that the dress is intended for practical work. It fastens down the back with buttons of jet and turquoise. A larger similar button is attached at hip-level on both sides. From this point the dress is left open at the seams, the front just clearing the ground and the back trailing a little, but easy to turn up out of the way. The under-gown of turquoise-blue cloth clears the floor in front.

Shoes: The flat-soled shoes, hardly seen, are of black fabric.

Accessories: The woman carries a purse and some keys.

82. Woman with Silver Jug. 1490–1500

Hair: This does not show under the headdress.

Headdress: The hood is of black velvet turned back with white. A pleated fan-shaped frill comes forward over either cheek from the cap.

Garments: The black velvet dress fastens down the front from a small plain collar. The sleeves are close-fitting with goblet cuffs. The train of the dress is turned up and fastened to the back of the waist, showing the train of the under-gown of deep-blue silk.

Footwear: Part of one blue velvet shoe is seen.

Accessories: The woman carries a small silver jug with a lid.

83. Armourer. Opening Years of Sixteenth Century

Hair: This is cut to a 'bobbed' length and turned in a little at the ends.

Headdress: The flat-crowned black velvet hat has a small round brim and a scarlet plume curved over the top.

Garments: The under-doublet of yellow silk has a small frill round the neck, and long close-fitting sleeves and puffed over-sleeves of the same colour with bands of scarlet and black. Sleeveless 'bases' are worn over it, consisting of a close-fitting yellow bodice ornamented in a criss-cross pattern of black braid and small gilt ornaments, and a yellow skirt of padded pleats decorated in scarlet and black. The square neckline has edging of scarlet, with gilt ornaments on a yellow ground. The narrow belt is of black leather.

Hose: The hose are scarlet and form a complete garment reaching the waist.

Boots: These are of buff leather, ending in turned-over tops below the knees.

Accessories: The armourer is picking up broken wooden lances at a tournament.

84. Woman Breaking Sticks for Firewood. 1520

Hair: The hair is parted in the centre and hardly shows under the cap.

Headdress: The white linen hood has its lappets tied over the top of the head.

Garments: The woman wears a dress of mustard-yellow woollen stuff with black edging at the open neckline, which is filled by a white lawn partlet. The bodice is fitted and the skirt fairly full. The sleeves are puffed at the top with close-fitting black lower sleeves attached.

Footwear: Flat-soled black fabric shoes are worn.

Accessories: The woman is breaking twigs to be used for firewood.

85. Baker with Tray of Loaves. Early Sixteenth Century

Hair: The hair is cut to a 'bobbed' length.

Headdress: The cap of brown felt is shaped and moulded in a frequently worn fashion of the time.

Garments: The belted tunic is of buff-yellow cloth, with full upper sleeves and lower close-fitting ones of deep blue attached below the elbows.

Hose: The long hose are of the same blue as the lower sleeves.

Footwear: The shoes are of black buckskin and do not follow the very wide shape then in favour.

Accessories: The baker carries a tray of loaves on his shoulder.

86. Carpenter. Early Sixteenth Century

Hair: The straight hair is of 'bobbed' length.

Headdress: The carpenter wears a buttoned-back and flat-topped cap of black felt.

Garments: The short-skirted doublet of vermilion cloth has a padded chest and fastens down the front with black buttons. A black leather belt is worn. The plain sleeves end at the wrist. A leather apron is tied on at the waist.

Hose: The hose are yellow.

Shoes: The broad-toed shoes are of black leather.

Accessories: The carpenter carries a hammer and the right-angled piece of wood known as a square. He has a knife in his belt; attached to the apron is an iron ring on which to hang additional tools.

87. Woman with Bowl and Spoon (Italian Fashion). Early Sixteenth Century

Hair: This is hidden by the cap.

Headdress: The woman wears a cap of unbleached linen with a shallow crown gathered on to a band and a deep flounce all round. It is set back from the face.

Garments: Part of the skirt of an under-gown of a pale brick-orange colour, with a narrow green border, shows below the skirt of the over-gown which is pouched over a girdle (unseen) at the hips. It is of a deeper brick colour than the under-gown and has a narrow black border at the close round neckline, the vertical opening to admit the head (fastened), the short shoulder-sleeves, and the open side-seams of the skirt. The inner sleeves from shoulder to wrist are of the same colour as the dress, and are slashed to show the white cotton sleeves of the chemise. The turned-back cuffs of this are also seen.

Shoes: Flat slippers of green fabric with broad toes are worn.

Accessories: The woman carries a spoon and a bowl of broth.

88. Labourer with Hod for Carrying Water. Early Sixteenth Century

Hair: The hair is roughly cut to a 'bobbed' length.

Headdress: The man is wearing a wide-brimmed flat-crowned hat of dark mole-coloured felt.

Garments: The belted tunic is of dull red-brown woollen stuff.

Hose: His coarse hose of grey-brown wool are tied below the knees.

Shoes: His flat shoes are of brown buckskin and have broad toes.

Accessories: The man holds a hod for carrying water, which can be hoisted on his back. A bag of unbleached linen hangs at his belt and contains personal belongings or tools.

89 Cook with Primitive Apparatus. Early Sixteenth Century

Hair: The hair is cut fairly short.

Garments: The man wears a shirt with sleeves rolled up, a green belted tunic, an apron tied low and full breeches of mole-coloured plush fabric.

Hose: The stockings are of grey-brown wool.

Shoes: The shabby shoes are of brown buckskin.

Accessories: The iron cooking-pot is set on a fire of small logs. The cook holds a long-handled skillet with collops of meat in it.

90. Mason. 1530–40

Hair: The hair is cut short and combed downwards all round the head, forming a short fringe over the forehead.

Garments: The collar of the white shirt has two rows of small frills into which the material of the shirt is gathered. The doublet of grey cloth ends at the waist and has full sleeves tapering from the forearm to the wrist. Its front, bordered in black and white, appears in the opening of the jerkin over the chest. This is of scarlet cloth with a long collar of black plush velvet whose ends meet just above the waist. Slashes on the shoulders and chest are paned with black. The skirt of the jerkin is hidden by a white apron which has been turned up to form a large pocket. The moderately full black breeches end in bands at mid-thigh.

Hose: The long hose are white.

Shoes: The flat broad shoes of black leather have practically no uppers, but just cover the base of the heels and the ends of the toes.

Accessories: The mason carries some tools of his trade.

91. Peasant Woman with Rake. About 1540

Hair: This is covered by the headdress.

Headdress: The head, chin, and shoulders are covered by a white cotton wimple. A flat-crowned wide-brimmed straw hat is worn over it.

Garments: The rolled sleeves of the white cotton chemise are visible. A square-topped bodice of rust-coloured woollen fabric, with shoulder-straps, has a skirt attached. This is folded and turned under at the hips. Two more skirts, one over the other, are worn, the lower one of brown cloth being longer than the upper one of green hempen stuff.

Hose: Stockings of grey yarn are rolled down to the ankles.

Shoes: Flat-soled mules of black leather are worn.

92. Tradesman's Wife in *Bongrâce* Headdress. About 1540

Hair: The hair is bound up at the back of the head. A curl hangs down on each side of the face.

Headdress: The flat square cap of black velvet resembles the *bongrâce* headdress, but has a short flap of velvet on each side, attached to the black caul or net which encloses the hair.

Garments: The under-dress, composed of a bodice and kirtle, is of green silk-faced stuff with long close-fitting sleeves which have narrow white wrist-frills. The kirtle is made in padded pleats for warmth, and is trimmed with two bands of black velvet. It is clear of the ground. The over-dress of orange cloth has a slightly high waist (a German style) to the fitted bodice. The round, fairly full skirt ends above the ground. The white pleated partlet is drawn into a black velvet band ornamented with gilt beads. The short puffed sleeves have bands and panes of black velvet. Attached to them are three-quarter length over-sleeves of doubled material, a reduced version of the large turned-back over-sleeve also in fashion.

Shoes: The shoes follow the natural shape of the foot and are of fawn buckskin.

Accessories: The woman carries a basket and is lifting her skirt preparatory to opening a black purse ornamented with three gilt tassels, attached to her kirtle at the waist.

93. Messenger or Courier. 1550–60

Hair: The hair is cut short and only a little of it is seen under the cap.

Headdress: The round beret-shaped cap of dark-green velvet has a small brim and a yellow plume on the left side.

Garments: The man wears a dark-green doublet with a high collar edged with a small ruff, and wrist-frills on the plain sleeves which have a strip of yellow braid down the outer side. Over it is a sleeveless buff leather jerkin. The round-hose are of dark-green cloth paned in yellow.

Hose: The hose are yellow.

Footwear: Thigh-length natural leather riding-boots are worn.

Accessories: The man wears a sword at his left hip and carries gloves in his right hand.

94. Chamberlain or Marshal of a Noble Household. 1560–70

Hair: The hair on the head is cut short. The beard and moustache are very long.

Headdress: The brimmed hat of black velvet has a fairly high stiffened crown arranged in vertical pleats and is decorated by a jewelled brooch and an aigrette.

Garments: The chamberlain wears a doublet of purple velvet and a short gown of brocade in gold, black and violet, worn over the shoulders with the sleeves left hanging. It has a large collar of white fur continuing into long revers. The fur lining shows in a narrow border at the hem and sleeve-ends.

Hose: The hose are of yellow silk.

Shoes: The shoes are of purple velvet, with a decoration of small slashes.

Accessories: He carries a wand of office.

95. Youth Selling Grapes. 1565

Hair: The hair is black and curling, cut fairly short.

Garments: The youth wears a jerkin of faded turquoise-blue over a dark wine-coloured shirt with its sleeves rolled up. His dull-red breeches end below the knees and are shaped at this point to provide a piece of stuff to kneel on.

Footwear: His legs and feet are bare.

Accessories: A large basket of grapes stands beside him.

96. French Serving-Woman. About 1570

Hair: The hair is puffed out a little at the sides from a centre-parting. At the back, under the cap, it is put up in a flat chignon or crossed swathes.

Headdress: The white linen cap is arched over the brow, dipping a little in the centre in front. At the back of the head its folds devolve into a short hanging veil.

Garments: The dress is of violet-grey wool. It has a low front to the bodice, filled in by a white lawn partlet with a round neckline. The bodice is a little high-waisted and has plain sleeves to the wrists. The full skirt ends at the instep. A white apron is worn.

Shoes: These are of fawn-grey leather, hardly seen.

Accessories: The woman carries a tray with a goblet on it.

97. French Peasant. 1577

Hair: This is cut in a rough uncurled 'bobbed' shape.

Headdress: The man wears a fawn-coloured felt hat with a flat brim and a tall, rounded crown. A green feather is worn on the left side.

Garments: His tunic of dark blue-green woollen stuff fastens down the front and has a flat open collar, showing the neck of the white shirt. It is belted at the waist and has sleeves to the wrists. Drawers of unbleached linen are partly seen.

Hose: The stockings are of green wool and are rolled below the knees.

Shoes: These are of black leather, the uppers being partly white.

Accessories: The man has a long narrow sack over his shoulder. It has two openings so that it can be filled at both ends and carried in this way. He also carries a wooden tray with a curved handle across the top, holding two cheeses. He has a knife in his belt.

98. French Peasant Woman. 1577

Hair: This is parted in the centre and put up in a knot fairly high at the back of the head.

Headdress: A straw hat with a flat-topped crown and a large brim is worn.

Garments: The dress of thin light-green wool has a fitted bodice, open down the front, with tucks of white linen filling in the opening and a white collar laid flat at the sides of the square neckline. The sleeves are long and plain. The skirt is pouched over an unseen girdle at hip-level, so that the dress does not come below calf-level.

Hose: The stockings are of grey yarn.

Shoes: The shoes are of black leather with a fastening over the instep.

Accessories: The woman carries a long stick over her shoulder, with a basket of vegetables suspended at one end of it and a second containing live ducklings at the other.

99. French Serving-Man in a Nobleman's House. 1584

Hair: The hair is curled into a longish 'bobbed' shape. A curled quiff stands up over the forehead.

Garments: The doublet of buff-yellow cloth, banded with ruchings of crimson silk, has shoulder-rolls and an exaggerated downward point in front in the 'peascod-belly' fashion. The trunk sleeves are of parchment-coloured silk slashed in crimson. A falling ruff and turned-back hand-ruffs of parchment-tinted lawn are worn. The narrow belt is of crimson leather. The artificial trunk-hose, which form merely a short basque or skirt, are of buff-yellow cloth with narrow bands of shot silver and crimson galloon. The sleeved cloak, worn slung over the right shoulder, is of crimson velvet, with shoulder-rolls and collar matching the body of the doublet and sleeves matching the artificial trunk-hose. The lining is of parchment-coloured silk.

Hose: The hose are of parchment-coloured silk and are made like tights, forming a complete garment.

Shoes: The flat shoes with rounded toes are of crimson velvet.

Accessories: The man carries a silver dish on which is a pie.

100. Italian Waiting-Gentlewoman. 1585

Hair: The hair is dressed smoothly with a centre-parting and does not show much under the cap.

Headdress: The halo-shaped headdress of black velvet ornamented in gold thread has some of the characteristics of the French hood.

Garments: The sleeveless dress is of shot silk in bronze and steel-colour, striped in vermilion. It has a slightly high waist and a square neckline outlined in black velvet. The lace partlet filling in the neckline has a high collar. The white lawn chemise-sleeves are visible.

Footwear: Only part of one red velvet shoe is seen.

CHAPTER FIVE
1590–1660

Elizabeth I had brought wages and prices under national control to be enforced by Justices of the Peace, instead of being in the hands of municipal authorities. Every craftsman had to spend seven years in perfecting his knowledge under a master. The coinage, debased under Henry VIII, had been restored by means of gold and silver acquired from Spanish America. The growth of overseas trade was an important social change in the time of Elizabeth.

Mining was developed with the help of German miners imported to work in the Lake District and the Mendips. Tin, lead, copper, coal, iron and salt were dug and exported, or used for home industries.

In the opening years of the seventeenth century, the wish to expand overseas was expressed in the determination to colonise extensively in parts of America. Noblemen, gentry and merchants of the City of London Companies found the money to promote the establishment of a permanent market in America to exchange goods, such as Virginian tobacco for English produce. The Virginia Company and the Massachusetts Bay Company were formed for the purpose, and between 1630 and 1643 financed the emigration of twenty thousand men, women and children in two hundred ships to New England, with forty thousand more to Virginia, Maryland and the West Indies.

Very many of them died on the hazardous journey through shipwreck or disease, and those who arrived were subject to attacks from Indians, and hardships of cold and privation. In New England, they settled and established a Puritan democracy under English common law. The English government had done little for the emigrants beyond sending out convicts, Negro slaves, and kidnapped youths taken overseas by force to serve a term of bondage before being freed to find a place in the new society. The settlers felt therefore they owed submission to no-one, political or ecclesiastic.

The traditions of the English landowner were carried on in the life of the Virginian plantations, where tobacco-growing became the staple industry. The planter, acting as overlord, magistrate, employer and arbiter of the lives of his dependants, was in the same position as the lord of an estate at home.

The ports of Liverpool and Bristol were used as clearing-stations for Negro slaves on their way to America, and as commerce developed between England and the colonies, the Navy protected the monopoly of trade and prevented piracy.

The East India Company, founded in 1600 by Elizabeth's charter, was given no such protection of its ships. These vessels, the great East Indiamen, were mounted with guns to keep at bay their trading rivals—the Portuguese and the Dutch, who had their own East India Company. On land, the Company paid a private army to defend its trading-stations and factories at Madras and Bombay, which it held by treaty with native princes. Employees were under the rule of the Company, which held full judicial power over them. Their trade extended to China and by overland route to Persia. The East India fleet was thirty strong in the early seventeenth century, and those ships that made the year's journey between India and the Thames, with cargoes of saltpetre, raw silk and spices, brought a knowledge of distant lands and an understanding of maritime affairs which increased the City's thirst for mercantile adventure.

Large houses in London and other towns still had gardens, but most had none and the buildings were tall and narrow, of different styles jostling one another and with attic storeys almost meeting across the street.

The duties of the seventeenth-century housewife were as demanding as in previous centuries. The lady of a manor-house, however, now had fewer gentlepeople around her, for the custom of keeping a large household of guests and dependants was dying out. There had been fewer gentlefolk helping in the house at the end of the sixteenth century, and by the middle of the seventeenth, paid servants had taken over most of the work. Only in royal households and in those of the higher nobility were the posts in the upper ranks still occupied by men of good family.

The age of the late Shakespearean tragedies, of Milton, of Rubens and Rembrandt, and the beginning of opera coincided with one of bestial cruelty and destruction. In the Netherlands, France and Germany, there were religious wars and persecutions—in England there was Civil War, disrupting and disastrous. The struggle between King and Parliament was one of conflicting and irreconcilable ideas; on the one hand, the King's inflated idea of his own royal prerogative, and on the other, the growing urge towards democracy and fear of despotism. This struggle was not finished until the country had exhausted itself, and experimented with Commonwealth and Protectorship. In 1660, Charles II restored the Stuart reign.

COSTUME OF THE PERIOD: 1590–1660

Hair—Men: Longer hair was worn in the 1590s than in the preceding decade. After 1600 it was worn at collar or shoulder level. Puritan influence induced a shorter cut, but a 'bobbed' length was often preferred to a shorter crop. Moustaches and short pointed beards or 'lip-tufts' were worn.

Hair—Women: The coiffure was tall and narrow at first, but grew wider in the early 1600s, taken back in a semicircular shape. It was dressed more closely to the head from the '30s to the '60s, with a chignon at a middle or high level, and sometimes a fringe of short spaced-out curls in front. Ringlets were seldom worn with practical dress.

Headdress—Men: The buttoned cap was still seen with some changes in the early years on peasants and craftsmen.

The *copotain* and the 'sugar-loaf' hat, resembling the *copotain* but with a rounded crown, were worn until the last quarter of the century, and by the unfashionable until the final decade. There were variations in the size and flexibility of the brim. The tall-crowned, wide-brimmed hat favoured by Puritans was one of its styles. The large-brimmed Cavalier hat of beaver, felt or velvet was worn by working people from about 1625, again with many different manipulations of the brim and with very little decoration, until the 1680s. The so-called 'night-cap' was worn indoors by gentry, and both indoors and outdoors by citizens and craftsmen. It had a rounded crown with a close-fitting rim turned up all round.

Headdress—Women: The French hood and the Marie Stuart cap (now considerably wider) and the *bongrâce* headdress were seen until about 1630. A wide arched hood, generally ending at the shoulders in practical dress, was in use until the 1640s. Loosely fitting hoods tied under the chin were sometimes wired to give a square or curved effect in front. They could be worn over caps of white lawn, muslin, lace and embroidery.

The *copotain* and 'sugar-loaf' hats in their numerous adaptations and the Cavalier hat with very little adornment, were also worn by women. A very small cap was put on over the chignon from the early years until the 1670s.

Garments—Men: The doublet was long-waisted at first, with a deep, slightly protuberant point or curve in front above the basque, and the join between body and basque higher at the back. The basque was narrow and could be cut in six or eight slightly overlapping tabs. These grew deeper and the waistline higher between 1610 and 1630. By then it was no longer pointed and the garment had become tight-chested. The high waistline could be indicated by bows or small rosettes.

By 1635 the doublet curved in a little at the waist and flared towards the hem, which now need not have a basque. A little of the shirt could be seen below it in many instances.

The upstanding or falling ruff was worn until about 1645. A wide collar reaching to the shoulders or a narrower one on a small neck-band took its place. These, with the square-cut Spanish *golilla* collar, with edges meeting in front but no ties, were the most usual forms of neckwear as the ruff was worn less often.

The sleeve was only moderately full in the 1590s, and during the decade most sleeves became close-fitting, with turned-back cuffs. Shoulder-rolls were worn until about 1640, and later by those who had few new clothes. Hanging sleeves were seen until about 1625, and until mid-century in children's dress. A sleeve full at the top and narrow from elbow to wrist had slashing and paning in the upper part. A fairly full sleeve, open from the upper arm to the wrist or ending at the forearm with the shirt-sleeve partly visible, was in fashion from 1635 to mid-century.

The leather jerkin was worn until it became a solely military garment about 1620. Long 'trunk-hose', with most of the fullness just above the knees, were worn until this date.

A short bolero jacket, with sleeves showing most of the shirt-sleeves and with the shirt visible at the waist, was worn with 'Dutch' breeches in the 1650s and '60s. These were narrow and tubular, ending below the knee or at the calf. 'Venetians', worn as practical dress, were not heavily padded on the hips but were plain breeches fastening below the knees. They were worn between 1600 and 1610 and again in the 1640s. 'Cloak-bag' breeches were of moderate fullness, sewn into bands just above the knees. 'Spanish hose', worn between 1630 and 1650, had a high waistline and tapered to a fastening below the knees.

From 1630 breeches were attached to the inner edge of the doublet by hooks and metal rings. They were not attached when the shirt was visible at the waistline, but made so that they kept in place at hip-level. Vertical side-pockets were made from about 1600. Both long riding-cloaks and short cloaks were worn.

Garments—Women: The feminine doublet ending at the hips, with or without a basque and slightly fitted to the figure, was worn with a ruff and sleeves full in the upper part and close-fitting from elbow to wrist or long and tight throughout. It could be worn with petticoats or a narrow farthingale beneath the separate kirtle which cleared the ground. All farthingales were out of fashion by 1625–30.

By the late 1620s and '30s the bodice was slightly high-waisted and attached to the skirt, with a long stomacher and sometimes a ribbon belt. The waistline was normal in the 1640s and '50s. A collar or partlet up to the throat was usual among Puritan adherents. Three-quarter length or full-length sleeves, of moderate fullness, accompanied this dress in the '40s and '50s.

Skirts that did not clear the ground were bunched up, showing a kirtle or petticoat that ended at the top of the shoes.

Hose and Stockings—Men: These were of wool yarn or cotton in neutral colours such as grey, fawn or brown, also black with sombre dress. Thick stirrup-hose, with a strap under the foot, were worn under boots for riding.

Footwear—Men: After 1625 the toes of men's shoes were square at the ends instead of being rounded. This fashion remained until after 1700. 'Shoe-roses' and ribbon-ties were unobtrusive on shoes for practical use. Flat-soled 'mules' were worn. Close-fitting boots ending above the knees had flat heels, slightly squared toes and oblong spur-leathers. Others ended at the top of the calf and had moderate-sized cup-shaped tops or larger ones, 'bucket-tops', turned up at mid-calf. They could have 'butterfly' spur-leathers and small low heels.

Stockings—Women: These were like those of men and were kept up by garters.

Shoes—Women: These resembled those of men. Wooden clogs and pattens with leather straps over the insteps were worn, also shoes raised on cork heels and flat-soled mules.

Materials, Colours and Ornament: Neutral brown, fawn or greyish tones, with dull reds, blues, greens, yellows, rust-colour and black, were worn. Buttons, slashing, rosettes, ribbon-loops and scarlet linings provided some colour. Doublet and breeches seams were trimmed with braid and caps, cuffs and collars of lawn or muslin with embroidery. Hatbands were of cord or leather.

101. Man in Furred Gown. 1590s

Hair: The hair is cut short and is hardly seen. A moustache and trimmed beard are worn.

Headdress: A black coif, not tied under the chin, is covered by a black velvet cap with a narrow rim.

Garments: The gown is of black velvet, edged all round with light-brown fur, which also edges the artificial hanging sleeves. The doublet is of deep-red cloth barred with silver stripes. The turned-down collar and the narrow cuffs are edged with lace. The basque is short and the round-hose below it of black velvet paned in red are artificial. The combination of coif, cap and furred gown is suitable as a costume for a magistrate, a civic dignitary, a doctor, scholar or other eminent or learned man.

Hose: The canions are of red silk, and red silk hose continue to the waist and take the place of breeches.

Shoes: These are of black reversed calf.

102. Woman in Arched Hood. Merchant's Wife. 1590s

Hair: The hair is taken up and back from the forehead, showing the ears because of the headband that holds the headdress in position.

Headdress: The collar forms part of this, as it rises from the V-shaped opening of the gown to a point near the top of the head, helping to support the arched hood. The collar is of stiffened black velvet, with a similar white lawn collar laid over it, so that only a narrow edge of black is seen. A narrow black velvet band is fastened across the hair and the arched hood or veil of stiffened white gauze is attached to this. It surrounds the head and collar and is fastened together at the collar-opening. It hangs down to the waist at the back.

Garments: The black velvet gown, trimmed with bands of silver braid on the bodice, skirt and sleeves, is worn over a small 'wheel' farthingale with fluted segments of velvet standing out round the waist of the dress. The sleeves are long and plain, with small shoulder-wings and turned-back lace cuffs.

Shoes: Only the tip of one black velvet shoe is seen.

103. Italian Fruit-Seller. 1590s

Hair: The hair is dressed close to the head, swept up all round to a small knot at the top of the head. Some small ringlets hang near the forehead and temples.

Headdress: A small ornament of red ribbon and beads is worn on the top of the head.

Garments: The white cotton or linen chemise can just be seen at the bodice-opening. Over it is a white linen blouse, open in a V-shape in front with a pleated ruff-collar lying flat on the shoulders. The sleeves are full at the top with loose plain lower sleeves attached below the elbows. Red shoulder-ribbons are worn. The yellow velveteen skirt has a figured-fitting bodice in green, fastening in front. The full skirt ends just above the shoes. The apron is of thick blue-green cotton or linen stuff, with a double border of red and green worked with gold thread, and a fringe of red, green and gold.

Footwear: The flat, rather thick-soled shoes of red fabric have high vamps (unseen) in the Elizabethan fashion.

Accessories: The fruit-seller is carrying a basket of peaches resting on leaves on her arm, and a wooden container holding a melon and some hazel-nuts in her left hand.

104. Woman Holding 'Bolster' Farthingale. 1590s

Hair: This shows only a little in front under the cap.

Headdress: The elderly serving-woman wears a white linen cap, curved round the face in front and with a *liripipe* hanging to shoulder-length at the back.

Garments: The dress of grey cloth has plain sleeves with a little fullness, a fitted bodice and a full skirt just clearing the floor. A small white ruff and red-and-grey shoulder-rolls are worn.

Shoes: These are of grey buckskin, with low heels.

Accessories: The woman is carrying a 'bolster' farthingale for her mistress to put on. She wears a leather pouch at her waist.

105. Wife of Wealthy Flemish Merchant. Early 1600s

Hair: This is hidden under the headdress.

Headdress: The flat-crowned black velvet hat has a cap-shaped piece of material under its rim to fit the head. Beneath this a plain white linen coif is worn.

Garments: A large French farthingale supports a skirt of yellow cloth, decorated with bands of black velvet and bordered with brown fur. An open, pleated skirt of yellow silk is worn over it. The apron is of green silk, with a broad band of black silk at the top and narrow black borders. The open black velvet bodice has a collar and edging of brown fur. Narrow bands of black velvet hold the bodice together over the white lawn chemise. The puffed sleeves of black velvet have close-fitting lower sleeves attached. A white ruff fits the neck closely.

Shoes: The tip of one black velvet shoe can be seen.

Accessories: The merchant's wife carries a pair of yellow and black fringed gloves.

106. Beggar. Early Seventeenth Century

Hair: The man's thinning hair is blown about by the wind. He wears an untrimmed beard and moustache.

Headdress: He carries his battered black felt hat in his hand, upturned to receive alms.

Garments: The faded greenish-grey doublet and full breeches, fastened below the knees, are torn and crumpled as is the dirty white linen collar.

Hose: Clumsy grey leather leggings cover his legs from below the knees to the ankles.

Shoes: The broken shoes are so dirty that the original light-brown colour can hardly be seen.

Accessories: The man carries a stick fashioned from a rough piece of wood.

107. Flemish Gardener. Early Seventeenth Century

Hair: This is straight and cut fairly short.

Headdress: The man wears a round black felt cap coming down over the ears.

Garments: The white shirt-sleeves are rolled up and the loose rust-coloured jerkin worn over them is sleeveless. The dull-green breeches have long tabs at the knees, used for kneeling upon.

Stockings: These are of green yarn.

Shoes: Stout black leather shoes are worn.

Accessories: The man is digging with a spade.

108. Spanish Labourer. Early Seventeenth Century

Hair: The hair is fairly short, showing only a little under the cap.

Headdress: The man wears a version of the buttoned-back cap in green felt.

Garments: The doublet is of brown leather trimmed at the sleeve-ends, collar and hem with tabs of its own stuff. The 'Dutch' breeches are ornamented in the same way.

Hose: The stockings, seen between the breeches and the boots, are of thick light-brown wool.

Boots: These end below the knees and have the same decoration as the garments.

Accessories: The man is wielding a pick-axe.

109. Highland Woman. Early Seventeenth Century

Hair: The hair is worn loose, but is almost covered by the plaid.

Headdress: The plaid covers the head, but a ribbon can be seen bound round the brow. It is tied (unseen) on the left.

Garments: The woman wears a dark-red dress with a fitted bodice and plain sleeves. It ends above the ankles. Her red-and-white plaid has been laid over her head and back with a belt buckled round it, leaving room for the movement of her arms and wrapping her body for warmth. It is fastened over the chest with a brooch.

Footwear: Her feet are bare.

110. Public Post-Messenger. About 1613

Hair: This is cut in a 'bobbed' shape, covering the ears. A moustache and small beard are worn.

Headdress: The black felt hat is a large-brimmed *copotain* with a band of scarlet and light green.

Garments: The post-messenger wears an old-fashioned doublet of scarlet cloth, with dark-green sleeves tied in by points under shoulder-rolls of scarlet and light-green. A scarlet stripe runs down the outside of the sleeve. The collar is a 'falling-band' of white linen, starched but not pleated, with matching cuffs. The natural-leather belt is to accommodate a sword when needed. The breeches are of dark-green cloth, fastened into bands below the knees. The scarlet ties are visible.

Stockings: The stockings are of green wool.

Shoes: These are of buff leather with flat soles, short tongues and laces tied over the insteps.

Accessories: The messenger has a leather bag for letters slung on a strap from his left shoulder to his right hip. He carries a staff with a knob that can be unscrewed, so that a confidential or important written message can be carried in the hollow top of the staff.

111. Townswoman. 1626

Hair: The hair shows only a little under the cap.

Headdress: A tall-crowned black felt hat with a wide brim is worn.

Garments: The woman wears a feminine form of the doublet in dark-green cloth. The sleeves are full at the top and close-fitting from elbow to wrist. She wears a white apron. Her fairly full skirt clears the ground. She wears a white ruff.

Shoes: Black leather shoes with moderate heels are worn.

Accessories: The purse is carried by its strings in the right hand and a red leather bag decorated in green, in which to put her purchases, in the left.

112. Pedlar. About 1630

Hair: The hair is roughly cut and long enough to cover the back of the neck.

Headdress: The large battered Cavalier hat of dark-green felt has two broken plumes, one light green and one red.

Garments: The white shirt is patched under the arm. The breeches are of dark rust-coloured cloth, torn and patched, with tattered ties below the knees. A doublet is slung by cords over the shoulders. It is of ragged dark-green velvet, paned in orange, with a torn white linen collar.

Stockings: These are of light-brown wool, badly shaped and wrinkled.

Shoes: The shoes of natural leather have bedraggled 'roses' of red ribbon.

Accessories: The pedlar has a tray of goods for sale slung round his neck on a leather or webbing strap. He has hung necklaces of artificial jewellery on his wrist and put many cheap rings on his fingers to show to his customers.

113. Milkmaid. 1630s

Hair: Curls over the forehead and at the sides of the head can be seen.

Headdress: The plain white lawn cap is turned back in front and has streamers attached which can be tied over the head. They are knotted at the back of the neck.

Garments: The bodice of the dress is in doublet form, with a deep, stiffened basque. It is open in front, with horizontal folds of white lawn covering the corset and others at the sides over the bosom. The flat white lawn collar lies on the shoulders and has long narrow ends coming down to the waist. Over-sleeves end at the elbow and the full-length inner-sleeves have turned-back white lawn cuffs. Bodice and over-skirt are of sapphire-blue cloth, with a narrow black sash to the former and two lines of black braid edging the skirt. The under-skirt is of pale-blue sateen with a triple border of dark-blue braid.

Shoes: The flat-soled shoes are of blue leather tied with black ribbon.

Accessories: The milkmaid is carrying a large pottery jug of milk on her head.

114. Printer or Engraver. About 1635

Hair: The hair is long and slightly curled.

Headdress: The man wears a conical cap of red felt.

Garments: The sleeveless buff jerkin has a wide flat collar and is fastened down the front. The white shirt-sleeves are rolled up. The breeches of brown cloth end below the knees. A short white apron is worn.

Hose: The stockings are of buff-coloured wool.

Boots: The wide-topped boots are of natural leather.

Accessories: The man is engaged at a printing press.

115. Pot-Boy or Scullion. 1635

Hair: This is worn long and unkempt.

Garments: The boy wears a shirt of scarlet twill and dark-blue breeches of rough hempen stuff, tied with string round the knees.

Footwear: His legs and feet are bare.

Accessories: He carries a large pottery jug with a small neck.

116. Youth with Viola. About 1640

Hair: The hair is cut moderately short and comes forward over the brow in short locks.

Headdress: The hat of light-brown felt is set well back on the head and at an angle, with the right side and the front of the brim turned up. A large part of the brim droops on to the left shoulder.

Garments: The white shirt is open down the front and the white pleated falling-band or ruff, also unfastened, fans out on to the shoulders. The shirt has lost the lower part of its sleeves. The boy wears an old leather buff jerkin with sleeves too short for him, and full breeches of a dark mole-colour, ending in bands below the knees.

Hose: The unfastened hose are of wrinkled and shabby grey-brown leather.

Shoes: The boy is wearing odd shoes. On the left foot is a brown buckskin shoe with a rounded toe and a strap across the instep. On the right is one with a high vamp, a tongue and a ribbon tie.

Accessories: The youth is a poor musician and plays the viola at gatherings or in the street.

117. Housewife. 1640s

Hair: The hair is taken back from the forehead with a chignon at mid-level (unseen) and curls at the sides.

Headdress: She wears a white linen cap turned back in front.

Garments: Her under-dress is of lavender-coloured poplin with blue velvet trimming, ending at the shoes. The over-dress is of dark pinkish-red in fine wool, turned up for freedom of movement. The fitted bodice has a stomacher of black velvet bars with a bow in the centre, showing the front of the white chemise. A white lawn partlet covers the neck-opening, with small bead ornaments round its close-fitting neck. A wide white linen collar, not meeting in front, extends to her shoulders. 'Virago' sleeves in a modified form are tied with black velvet and show the sleeves of the white chemise. The lower sleeves are of the same stuff as the over-dress. Their white linen turned-back cuffs end above the wrists.

Stockings: The housewife wears white stockings (unseen).

Shoes: The shoes are of black reversed calf with fairly high heels. They are tied over the instep.

Accessories: Some keys attached to a cord at the waist of the dress indicate the wearer's status as the wife of a moderately wealthy householder.

118. Man in Puritan Dress. 1640s

Hair: The hair is not cropped, but worn at a short 'bobbed' length.

Headdress: A wide-brimmed hat of black felt is worn. Its tall crown diminishes towards the top.

Garments: The man wears a grey cloth 'jump' jacket and matching Dutch breeches. These are piped in black with black buttons at the outside of the knees. The collar is of white linen cut in a square shape. Plain white cuffs are worn. The short black cloak is lined with scarlet.

Stockings: These are of grey wool.

Boots: 'Bucket-top' boots of natural-coloured leather are worn. They have large spur-leathers on the vamps.

119. Woman in Puritan Dress. 1640s

Hair: This is hidden by the cap.

Headdress: A white lawn cap with a frill round the face is tied on under the chin. A wide-brimmed black felt hat with a tall diminishing crown is worn over it.

Garments: The plain slate-blue woollen dress has a fitted bodice with an insertion of white lawn pleats in the centre of the front. The circular skirt just clears the ground. A plain white linen collar and cuffs are worn, also a white apron.

Footwear: The squared-off toe of one black leather shoe can be seen.

Accessories: The woman carries a small devotional book.

120. Irishman. Second Quarter of Seventeenth Century

Hair: This is worn long, reaching the shoulders, and is brought forward in a fringe over the forehead.

Garments: The man is wrapped in a large cloak of loosely woven Irish woollen stuff in light brown. Beneath this can be seen the V-shaped neck of a shirt of thick terra-cotta coloured linen. The close-fitting trews are light green, striped in red-brown. This costume illustrates some of the characteristics of native Irish dress which the Irish were forbidden to wear from the reign of Henry VIII to that of James I. They were ordered to wear the contemporary English costume. In the reign of Charles I they were allowed to wear their own dress again.

Footwear: The man wears natural leather shoes following the shape of the foot, like those worn in Elizabethan England.

Accessories: The man carries a staff.

121. Irishwoman. Second Quarter of Seventeenth Century

Hair: This is done in two plaits, one of which is brought forward over the left shoulder.

Headdress: A sort of turban of yellowish-fawn linen is worn.

Garments: The woman is wearing the large enveloping cloak that was one of the chief distinguishing features of the Irish dress of both sexes at this time. It was disliked by the English, who feared it might conceal weapons. It is of heavy green cloth, lined with brown fur which forms a big collar, and is held closely wrapped according to custom. She holds a baby in her arms, wrapped in the folds of the cloak.

Footwear: The plain, flat-soled natural leather shoes have fairly high vamps, like those worn in England a little earlier.

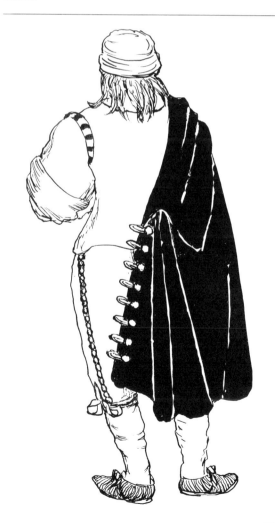

122. Artisan or Tradesman Wearing 'Night-Cap'. 1650

Hair: The hair is long and straggling, hanging loose to the shoulders.

Headdress: The man wears a round 'night-cap' of red cloth, turned up all round.

Garments: The short close-fitting doublet of dull-red woollen fabric has a round white collar. The matching breeches are 'Spanish' hose ending at the calves. They are ornamented with buttons along the outer seam. A cloak of mole-grey cloth hangs over the shoulder. It can be fastened on either side when worn over both shoulders.

Stockings: The stockings are of grey wool or yarn.

Shoes: The man wears red leather shoes with instep-ties.

123. Vagrant Woman. 1652

Hair: The hair is hidden by the cap.

Headdress: A head-fitting unbleached linen cap, now very dirty, is worn with the front turned down instead of back, as was more usual. The baby wears a makeshift bonnet of once light-coloured material.

Garments: The ragged dress is torn and filthy, reduced in colour to a mixture of undistinguishable faded tints. The baby is strapped to the woman's back by means of leather bands over her shoulders and a length of stuff wound round her neck and body. It is wrapped in an old piece of canvas blanket, but wears a little dress in a better state than that of the mother.

Shoes: Broken shoes of cracked natural leather are worn.

Accessories: The woman is counting her small store of money.

124. Housewife or Maidservant. 1658

Hair: The hair is drawn back from the forehead and dressed in a chignon at the crown of the head.

Headdress: A small cap of unbleached linen is worn over the chignon.

Garments: The boned bodice of tan-coloured cloth has lower sleeves of light brown, attached in the middle of the upper arm. Its rounded neckline discloses the round neck of the white linen chemise. The skirt of the dress is turned up all round showing a chestnut-brown lining, also a green underskirt just clearing the ground.

Shoes: The brown leather shoes, tied over the insteps, are partly seen.

Accessories: The woman is polishing a pewter jug with a lid.

125. Housewife or Female Attendant in Travelling-Cloak. About 1660

Hair: The curls over the forehead are all that can be seen of this. The front of a white lawn cap is visible.

Headdress: The limp loose hood of plum-coloured woollen stuff is attached to the shoulder-cape of the travelling-cloak.

Garments: The long full cloak is of plum-coloured cloth, piped in green, with apertures for the arms. The plain three-quarter length sleeves of the chemise, sewn into bands at the ends, can be seen.

Footwear: The front of one dark-green velvet shoe can be seen.

Accessories: The woman is holding a dark-green velvet purse with strings, decorated with pink flowers.

CHAPTER SIX
1660–1715

The Restoration of the Stuarts in England brought a certain amount of religious tolerance in its train. Charles II issued a writ in 1667 forbidding the killing of dissidents, so that actual bloodshed might be stopped. Sects such as the Quakers, however, met with physical ill-treatment, and some discrimination was exercised against Catholics and Puritan extremists in commerce and the taking of public office.

Charles and his associates set up the study of experimental science. The King was well aware of its use in industry, agriculture, medicine, engineering and navigation, and founded the Royal Society so that knowledge of it could be pursued. Scientific discoveries included Newton's improved telescope, the invention of a water barometer for forecasting the weather, improvements on early microscopes and methods of supplying air to divers.

Charles II also revived the theatre in London as an amusement for his Court. Drury Lane playhouse, now the Theatre Royal, was roofed in and had a drop-curtain, candle-lit foot-lights, and scenery painted in Baroque style. Women were allowed to act on the stage for the first time, and the music of Purcell and Lully was played. The works of Shakespeare, Ben Jonson, Beaumont and Fletcher, Ford, Massinger and Webster were put on, with the bawdy comedies of Wycherley and Aphra Behn, and the dramas of Dryden.

In the two major disasters of the century, the Great Plague and the Great Fire of London in 1665–6, a fifth of London's population was killed by the former and the whole of the City between the Tower and the Temple destroyed by the latter. In the rebuilding of the City merchants' houses, brick was used to replace the timber of the old Tudor buildings.

There were no banks, but money was carried by trusted employees to be locked up safely or lodged in the care of City goldsmiths. The first cheques were the notes written to gold-smiths asking them to pay out a designated sum from the amount held on a client's behalf. Loans were needed to improve land and for merchants to invest in home or foreign trade. A growing money market led eventually to the founding of the great banking houses.

Country houses had changed in character and were no longer built with an eye to defence. The central hall was replaced by separate dining and drawing rooms, a library, a morning-room, an estate room for the bailiff, a study for the master of the house and a boudoir for his lady. The kitchen itself was spacious as a rule, with a huge hearth, a turnspit and a wide chimney. Bacon was hung to cure in the wood-smoke. A still-room and larder would be adjacent, and a wine-cellar with butler's pantry nearby, with storage-places for wood, coal and charcoal.

In farmhouse kitchens, cottages, artisans' dwellings and the lesser manor-houses, an old-fashioned breakfast of ale or soup with meat or bread was still favoured. Among the gentry, small bread-rolls or little cakes might be eaten in the bedroom on rising. Chocolate, coffee or tea was drunk from handleless porcelain cups, brought to Europe by the English and Dutch East India Companies. Most well-found houses had silver vessels and platters as well as pewter. Spoons, knives and pronged forks, as well as fingers, were used for eating. Finger-bowls and napkins were changed frequently during a meal.

Walls had wainscoting and panelling, or dados with tapestry above. 'Table-carpets' were of silk, plush, velvet or tapestry. Deep wide fireplaces with ingle-nooks were to be found in manor-houses, and in many cases, there was a 'priest-hole' to one side of the hearth in which fugitives had hidden during the Civil War.

Among the occupations of the country house were the making of home-made wines—elderberry, cowslip, ginger, grape, currant and orange were some of them—and the distilling of scents and essences, washes for the hair and complexion, and the drying of lavender and pot-pourri. Fruits were candied or preserved in syrup, as were rose-petals and violets.

Coffee-houses were opened in London and became meeting-grounds for purveyors of gossip, business transactions and political discussion. Single news-sheets could be read there for a small fee from about 1704.

In 1685, Louis XIV revoked the Edict of Nantes, which had given the Huguenots protection. In the persecution that followed, many Protestants fled from France. Those who came to London settled for the most part in Soho, Long Acre and Spitalfields, where they worked at skilled trades, such as the weaving of silk. In this way, by the early eighteenth century, populous foreign quarters had been added to the area between St. Giles' Church and the Tower. In this district, lawyers, shopkeepers, financiers and the City merchants who controlled the trade between London and most of the known world lived and worked at close quarters with the thieves, cut-throats, harlots and coiners who inhabited the crowded tenements and alley-ways.

COSTUME OF THE PERIOD: 1660–1715

Hair—Men: 'Bobbed' and shoulder-length hair was worn by working men of most grades. A 'bobbed' wig to resemble this style was worn by clerical workers, craftsmen, tradesmen and elderly men. Those who dressed more formally wore the full-bottomed wig. After 1710 men's coiffure became smaller and dressed close to the head. They began to tie it back, and some examples of powdered hair were seen. Small horizontal curls were pinned up at the sides of the head.

Hair—Women: From about 1660 women's hair was usually drawn back into a moderate-sized chignon half-way up the back of the head. When hair was dressed high in front from the 1680s, that of working women was arranged in a roll or a curled fringe. Ringlets could show at the back or be bundled under the cap. Between 1710 and 1715 women's hair was swept up into the small neat Rococo coiffure, with a chignon on the top of the head.

Headdress—Men: Tall-crowned hats evolved from the *copotain* and the 'sugar-loaf' were worn until 1670. A hat with a low hard crown and moderate-sized brim was in use from 1665 for about ten years. The felt or 'beaver' hat with a rounded head-fitting crown and flexible brim, seen during many centuries, was in favour for practical work. Hats originating in the Cavalier type, but with narrower brims and little trimming, were worn straight on the head, turned up in front or at one or both sides in the 1670s and '80s. The cocked hat developed gradually into the tricorne between the late '80s and 1715.

The 'night-cap' was still worn by craftsmen, and indoors by gentry. Various woollen hats and caps were worn by working men.

Headdress—Women: A smoothly dressed uncovered head was usual at the opening of the period, with a ribbon or a tiny cap over the chignon. A hood tied under the chin was in use throughout. Caps were seen less often than formerly until the 1680s, when the *fontange* and the 'cornet' were worn with reduced decoration in working dress. The former was an early form of mob-cap, set back on the head with an upstanding frill in front. The latter had a small frill in front and a back lappet descending below the shoulders, with a 'topknot' of ribbon over the forehead. Shawls and scarves could be draped over these headdresses for going out.

Between 1710 and 1715 a round flat cap known as a 'pinner' came into use with the small neat coiffure. Little flower-trimmed hats were worn at an angle.

Garments—Men: The doublet, worn until approximately 1670, was still in use by less fashionable men. It was usually short, showing the shirt below its hem. Its sleeves ended just below or above the elbow, with a slit at that point.

'Petticoat' or 'Rhinegrave' breeches were worn with the short doublet in the 1660s. They were immensely wide breeches resembling a kilt in appearance. 'Dutch' breeches were worn as an alternative.

By 1670 a long loose coat and waistcoat had brought about a major change. The sleeves ended above the elbow, at the forearm or above the wrist, with large turned-back cuffs showing the wrist-frills and part of the shirt-sleeves. With the long sleeve worn with a sleeved waistcoat the latter might be turned back over the coat-cuff or, if the waistcoat were not worn, the coat-cuff itself turned back to show a different-coloured lining. The rounded neckline was collarless and the pockets set low.

By 1675 the coat was fitted to the figure and the skirt flared. From 1690 it had pleats on each side, stemming from the vents at the low waistline. Pockets could be set higher. By this date the waistcoat ended above the knees.

The 'jump', a plain long-sleeved jacket, was worn a great deal for practical work in the second part of the century.

The cravat, worn from about 1670, could be tied in a bow, linked at the throat by cravat-strings, or loosely knotted. The Steinkirk was a long, loosely twisted neckcloth, pulled through a button-hole near the top of the coat. It was worn from 1690 to 1730.

Breeches resembling full bloomers, pouched just below the knee, were worn from 1670. They diminished gradually until by 1690 knee-breeches had taken their place.

The Brandenburg, a loosely fitting overcoat, was worn more often than the cloak from 1690.

Garments—Women: In 1660 the bodice was long-waisted with a deeply pointed stomacher. Skirts were long and full, closed or open in front. They could be turned up in various ways showing an underskirt that cleared the ground.

From the 1670s a narrower skirt gave a more elongated line. The waistline could be rounded after 1680 and the skirt was drawn back into a kind of bustle. From 1710 the pyramidal early Rococo skirt, closed in front and with a circular hem, introduced a change.

The neckline throughout was low, square, oval or boat-shaped, usually covered in practical dress by a deep collar. An alternative was to show the top of the chemise above a rounded, moderate neckline.

Sleeves were usually three-quarter or elbow-length with turned-back cuffs, in some cases showing the chemise sleeve ending at the forearm. A sleeveless bodice, worn in some form throughout the period, showed the whole of this sleeve. Some long, tight sleeves were worn after 1710. The apron, plain or ornamental, was an integral part of women's dress.

Stockings—Men: Stockings were of yarn, wool, knitted jersey, cotton and worsted. Colours were grey, white, black, brown, ash-colour and some bright tints. Most were knitted, but tailored stockings of serge, canvas or linen and similar stuffs were still seen. Stirrup-hose in any of these materials were still worn.

Stockings—Women: These were like those of men.

Shoes—Men: Squared-off toes and raised heels were worn throughout the period. Shoes had high squared tongues and were fastened over the insteps with ribbons, small buckles and straps or buttons. They were made chiefly of black leather or cloth. Mules could have flat soles or slightly raised heels.

Boots—Men: Boots followed the shape of shoes in the part covering the foot. Heavy jack-boots could be pulled on, but lighter ones were fitted more closely, laced, buttoned or buckled down the outer side or front of the leg. Both were of thigh-length or had bucket-tops.

Shoes—Women: Women's shoes after 1660 had slightly squared or pointed toes and either flat or shaped heels, with long vamps with or without fastenings across the insteps. Their mules could have high or flat heels. Pattens and clogs were worn in bad weather.

Boots—Women: Long leather boots were worn for riding.

Materials, Colours and Ornament: The stuffs and colours used for practical dress remained the same as those mentioned in the preceding chapter, except that printed calico, cotton, linen and silk became obtainable for women's dresses. Ribbons, buttons and braid, with some lace and embroidery, were the chief means of ornament.

126. Country Girl or Maidservant. 1660

Hair: The hair is parted in the centre, with curls worn at the sides.

Headdress: A plain white linen cap fits across the back of the head.

Garments: The pale-yellow linen dress has a long stiffly boned bodice in the straight up-and-down fashion of the 1660s. It has a fairly wide skirt clearing the ground. A white apron is worn. The wide white linen collar covers the shoulders and is laced together in front. The plain loose sleeves end in turn-ups below the elbows in the same colour as the gown.

Footwear: The grey leather shoes have tongues with fastenings across them, and fairly high heels (unseen).

Accessories: She carries a bowl from which she is feeding ducks.

127. Inn Serving-Maid. 1660s

Hair: This is drawn back from the face and put up in a small chignon at mid-level at the back of the head.

Headdress: The cap of white linen fits over the chignon at the back and curves forward over the cheeks in front.

Garments: The pink bodice has a wide neckline which shows the top of the white chemise. The sleeves are long and plain. There is a deep basque ending just below the hips. The skirt of darkish-blue woollen fabric ends above the shoes.

Stockings: The stockings of grey cotton are hardly visible.

Shoes: The shoes of grey-brown reversed calf are tied over the insteps.

Accessories: The girl carries two large pottery jugs.

128. Estate-Bailiff or Land-Agent. 1660s

Hair: The hair is worn long, but not much curled.

Headdress: The hat of brown felt is carried in the hand. It has a diminishing crown and rolled brim, and is decorated by a green plume.

Garments: The man wears the equivalent in plain dress of the costume known as 'Rhinegrave' or 'petticoat' breeches. Originally designed as a riding-dress, its appearance differs from the elaborate ribbon-decked version worn by dandies. It has a bolero jacket with short sleeves showing a great deal of the white shirt-sleeves, which end in bands and short turned-down cuffs. The shirt-collar is turned down and tied in front. The breeches look like a kilt but are in fact divided. They match the jacket which is in green cloth bordered with orange. A pair of breeches in brown leather is worn as well.

Stockings: These are of light-brown wool.

Boots: These are of natural leather and end at the calves.

129. Dutch Serving-Maid. 1668

Hair: The hair is taken back from the forehead and is hardly seen.

Headdress: The cap of unbleached linen has a long turned-back front forming part of a lappet that goes round the cap. A small cap-shaped protuberance at the back covers the chignon.

Garments: The full skirt is of coarse orange-tan hempen fabric. Over it is worn a bodice with a very deep basque ending below the hips. This is of reddish-brown wool and has turned-back cuffs to the elbow-length sleeves. The apron is of unbleached cotton.

Shoes: The flat-soled shoes are of brown fabric.

Accessories: The girl is carrying a bunch of herbs.

130. Lawyer. 1668

Hair: The hair is of 'bobbed' length, smoothly dressed, with a quiff arranged above the forehead.

Garments: The long black gown touches the floor. It fastens in front with buttons set on a panel of its own material. There are artificial hanging sleeves with the plain black sleeves of the coat, which are actually worn, emerging from the arm-openings of the gown.

Footwear: Part of one black leather shoe is seen.

Accessories: The lawyer carries a book.

131. Country Girl with Bucket. 1670

Hair: This is parted in the centre and is almost hidden by the cap.

Headdress: The girl wears a folded and conical cap of un-bleached linen or wool.

Garments: The dress is of linen or soft woollen stuff in striped maroon and white. It has a wide flat collar of white linen and the bodice is laced over a white chemise. The elbow-length sleeves are turned back in white cuffs. The moderately full skirt hangs unevenly and ends at the ankles. A white bibless apron with a large pocket across the front of the skirt is worn.

Stockings: The stockings are of white cotton.

Shoes: The low-heeled shoes are of light-brown leather.

Accessories: The girl is carrying a wooden bucket bound with metal.

132. Man with Hand-Plough. 1670s

Hair: The hair is long, touching the shoulders, but not much curled.

Garments: The man wears a white shirt, open at the neck, and full dark-green breeches pouched over a band below the knee.

Stockings: These are of pale-grey cotton.

Shoes: The flat-heeled shoes are of fawn-grey buckskin.

Accessories: The plough is worked by dragging it along to make a furrow by hand.

133. Boy with Recorder. 1670s

Hair: The hair is moderately long and roughly cut.

Headdress: The boy wears an untrimmed green velvet Cavalier hat, shabby and out of fashion, set back on his head.

Garments: The coat is of blue-green cloth, fitting the figure closely and appearing a little too small. It fastens down the front and has a slightly flared skirt. The cream-coloured wrist-bands of the shirt are seen below the plain coat-sleeves. The breeches of dark plum-coloured plush are fairly full and sewn with bands below the knees. The boy wears a narrow cream-coloured cravat.

Stockings: The stockings are light grey.

Shoes: The brown leather shoes fasten over the instep.

Accessories: The boy, a strolling musician, is playing a recorder.

134. American Housewife with Baby Girl. 1674

Hair : Some curls on the forehead are all that can be seen of the mother's hair. The little girl's hair shows under the back of her cap.

Headdress : The mother wears the often-seen 'loose limp hood' of fine white lawn, tied on under the chin. The baby wears a white linen Puritan cap, turned back in front.

Garments : The gown of dark-blue grosgrain is made in the Puritan tradition. The bodice is fitted over a rigid corset without the deeply pointed stomacher of European dress at this time. The wide collar is of white lace. The sleeves are tied with dark-blue ribbons and the white muslin sleeves of the chemise are visible below them. The white muslin apron is embroidered. The baby wears a cream-coloured linen dress, with a white lawn apron and under-sleeves of white muslin.

Footwear : The toe of one of the mother's black leather slippers is visible. The baby's shoes are of white kid.

Accessories : The mother holds a baby's bottle. This is made to stand upright like an ordinary bottle, but has a specially shaped top.

135. Woman with Skirt Looped at the Back. 1675

Hair : This is bundled into the cap. A few curls can be seen below it.

Headdress : The back of the head is seen with the cap, an early version of the fontange, covering it. The upstanding frills in front are plain and not very large.

Garments : The fitted bodice of heavy pink cotton stuff has swathed bands of white muslin round its wide oval neck-line. These are decorated with small pink artificial flowers. The white muslin puffed sleeves of the chemise can be seen. The skirt of the over-gown is looped up and the central point of its hem pinned at the back of the waist. Part of the green and white underskirt is visible.

Stockings : The stockings are of white knitted kersey.

Shoes : Green leather shoes with raised heels and laced over the instep are worn.

136. Inn Serving-Maid. 1675

Hair: The hair is partially done up in a chignon at a fairly high level. Some strands, which bear signs of being curled, are allowed to hang down at the back.

Garments: The dress is of thick cotton or linen in reddish-purple. It has dropped from one shoulder and the sleeves are short with turned-back cuffs. The bodice is fitted to the figure and the skirt tucked under and fastened (unseen) at the waist at several points. A good deal of the ankle-length petticoat, striped in dark purple and flame-pink, is visible.

Footwear: The bare feet are thrust into flat-soled green leather mules.

Accessories: The girl carries a small empty barrel under her left arm and holds a jug in her right hand.

137. Seller of Broadsheets. 1680

Hair: The hair is raggedly cut to a length just below the ears.

Headdress: The large battered hat is of black felt. It has lost its original trimming, probably bunches of coloured ribbon on both sides.

Garments: The crumpled white cotton shirt has a buttoned neck-fastening but otherwise is wrapped together. Its cuffs are unfastened and without wrist-bands. The breeches, fastening below the knees with ragged ties, are of black cloth. The coat is of claret-coloured cloth. Some of its buttons and those that should be on the cuffs and pockets are missing.

Hose: The stockings are of wrinkled grey cotton.

Shoes: These are of grey reversed calf, now shabby, with tongues turned down over the vamps.

Accessories: The man holds some copies of a broadsheet in one hand and is holding out a specimen of them for sale.

138. Man in Brandenburg Coat. 1689

Hair: The natural hair hangs at the back in loose ringlets.

Headdress: The black velvet hat has a dented brim from much wear. The flat-topped crown is of medium height.

Garments: The loose calf-length coat is of putty-coloured cloth. It has loose sleeves with turned-back cuffs and has a square-cut collar at the back. In front, unseen, it is fastened by frogs. There is a vent in the back of the coat.

Stockings: The stockings are of thin grey-beige wool.

Shoes: The shoes of grey leather fasten over the instep.

Accessories: The man carries a sword.

139. Architect or Mason. About 1690

Hair: The hair is fairly long and is almost straight.

Headdress: The tall-crowned black felt hat has an upward-curving brim.

Garments: The architect wears a blue coat with three pleats at the sides concealing vents, and vertical pockets. The sleeves have large turned-back cuffs showing a little of the shirt-sleeves. His plain cravat is cream-coloured. The knee-breeches are of black plush. A white apron with a large pouch made out of its own width is worn.

Stockings: The stockings are of pale-grey cotton.

Shoes: The shoes are of dark-grey reversed calf and are fastened over the instep.

Accessories: The man is pointing with a short staff.

140. Man in Loose Overcoat. 1690

Hair: The hair is long enough to touch the collar.

Headdress: A black felt hat with an upturned brim is worn.

Garments: The loosely fitting coat of blue-grey cloth is of the 'Brandenburg' type. The sleeves have moderate-sized turned-back cuffs. The coat ends at the knees.

Stockings: The stockings are of thin pale-grey wool.

Shoes: These have small shaped heels and instep-fastenings. They are of grey-brown reversed calf.

Accessories: The man carries a cane.

141. Physician. 1690

Hair: The full-bottomed wig has thick curls over the forehead and at the bottom, but is left straight at the crown of the head and for part of its length at the back.

Garments: The long cloak, hanging open from the shoulders, is of wine-red velvet. A little of the suit of greyish-pink cloth can be seen.

Stockings: These are of pearl-grey silk.

Footwear: The doctor wears shoes of grey-fawn buckskin, with slightly raised and shaped heels and ties over the insteps.

Accessories: He carries a cane with a large silver knob. This is hollow and can be unscrewed to take out the pills it contains.

142. London Alderman. 1690s

Hair: The hair is long and loosely curled, with a quiff brushed up against the front of the cap.

Headdress: The round head-fitting cap is of scarlet felt or cloth.

Garments: The alderman's scarlet fur-edged robe is long at the back, trailing on the floor, and is worn over a coat resembling a lengthened-sleeved waistcoat. This lacks the large turned-back cuffs of the fashionable coat, but has white embroidered cuffs. It is of rich material in red, black and grey. Black knee-breeches are worn. The cravat is of ivory-coloured lace.

Stockings: These are of pearl-grey silk.

Shoes: The black leather shoes have large tongues with ribbon-ties over the insteps and raised shaped heels.

Accessories: The alderman carries his black felt wide-brimmed hat in his hand.

143. Lady's Maid. 1690s

Hair: The hair is rolled back over the brow. The remainder is covered by the cap.

Headdress: The bonnet-shaped cap is stiffly starched. It has goffered frills in front with cherry-red ribbon tied round the cap with a top-knot in front.

Garments: The dress is of fine-quality ivory-coloured linen, striped in cherry-red. The bodice fits the figure and has three parallel layers of plain ivory-coloured linen edging it from the shoulders to the waist. Within these an upstanding frilled collar of pleated matching and starched lawn surrounds the bosom. A bow of cherry-red ribbon is set below the front of the collar. The sleeves are three-quarter length with turned-back cuffs and ruffles. The skirt is formed into a draped bustle at the back and ends above the shoes. A cream-coloured lawn apron with a small bib is worn. There are vertically opening pockets on each side of the apron.

Footwear: The cherry-red fabric shoes have ties over the insteps and fairly high heels.

Accessories: A pair of scissors and a watch on a chain are attached to the waist-belt. The maid is in charge of her mistress's pet dog.

144. Boy Serving in Coffee-House. Early 1700s

Hair: The boy's natural hair is covered by a light-brown artificial-looking wig, of a type worn by the other servitors as well.

Garments: The cloth coat is of a pinkish-fawn colour and has three pleats at each side, starting from the low waist-line. The neckcloth is seen at the rounded collarless neck of the coat. The sleeves are plain, without the large turned-back cuffs of the current fashion. A white apron is half-tied at the back and tied securely in front.

Stockings: These are of light fawn-coloured wool.

Shoes: The light-brown shoes of reversed calf have ties over the insteps.

Accessories: The boy is carrying a tray holding a glass of wine and a coffee-cup without a handle or a saucer, such as were used at the time.

145. Cooper. Early Eighteenth Century

Hair: The natural hair covers the ears and touches the neckcloth at the back.

Headdress: The man wears a 'nightcap' of dark-green linen with an upturned border of buff-yellow.

Garments: The sleeved waistcoat is of dark-green woollen fabric. The knee-breeches are unseen, being covered by the voluminous apron of unbleached linen. The neckcloth is of plain white linen.

Stockings: These are of grey wool.

Shoes: Black leather flat-soled mules are worn.

Accessories: The cooper has a mallet in his right hand which he is using with a blunt-sided, possibly wooden implement, to knock the binding of the barrel into place.

146. Carpenter. Opening Years of Eighteenth Century

Hair: The hair is long and straight and worn loose, though it could be tied back.

Headdress: The 'night-cap' is of scarlet cloth, with a pointed top.

Garments: The man wears a sleeved waistcoat or 'jump' jacket of dun-coloured woollen fabric with long close-fitting sleeves open a little at the wrists. He wears a white apron and black plush knee-breeches.

Stockings: The stockings are of dun-coloured worsted.

Footwear: The flat-soled shoes are of natural leather, with tongue and buckles.

Accessories: The man is using a carpenter's plane.

147. Townswoman. About 1711

Hair: This shows a little under the headdress.

Headdress: The loose limp hood, a popular fashion, is surmounted by a flat-brimmed low-crowned black hat.

Garments: The woman wears a gown of pink poplin, with a shoulder-wide collar of white lawn with a white goffered frill round the edge. The short over-sleeves are turned up at the elbow and the white lawn sleeves of the chemise are seen below them.

Stockings: These are white cotton, unseen.

Footwear: The shoes are of dark-grey reversed calf, tied over the insteps.

Accessories: The woman is carrying a small lidded basket and a string bag containing fish.

148. Reaper. Early Eighteenth Century

Hair: The hair is cut in a short casual 'bobbed' shape.

Headdress: The small hat of brown felt has its brim turned up all round.

Garments: The crossed-over neckline of the white lawn shirt is visible. The short close-fitting 'jump' jacket is of green woollen fabric with close-fitting knee-breeches to match.

Stockings: The stockings are of thin light-brown wool.

Shoes: The shoes are of light-brown reversed calf and are fastened over the instep.

Accessories: The boy carries a hook and a small sheaf of corn.

149. Farm Boy. About 1715

Hair: The hair is of moderate length, reaching the collar.

Headdress: The green felt hat has a rounded brim turned up in front and a head-fitting crown.

Garments: The boy wears a brown woollen belted coat ending below the knees. It is plain and shabby, with sleeves to the wrists. His breeches are hidden by it.

Stockings: These are of wrinkled brown yarn.

Shoes: The shoes of brown reversed calf are much worn.

Accessories: The boy is leaning his chin on his crossed arms over the haft of a large agricultural fork.

150. Village Girl. About 1715

Hair: This is taken back from the forehead and pinned up in a fairly high chignon at the back, with some short curls hanging from it.

Garments: The girl wears a sleeveless bodice of green glazed cotton, with a wide neckline and tabs at the base. The puffed chemise-sleeves of white lawn are seen. The skirt is of cotton stuff, striped in terra-cotta and pale yellow. It is wide and circular, ending at the ankles.

Feet: The feet are bare.

Accessories: The girl is carrying a jar covered in wicker-work, probably of pottery and containing water.

CHAPTER SEVEN

1715–1780

This was a period of great development in the material conditions of society, and of the arts, philosophy and religion. The life of the labouring classes in town and country was still one of poverty and hardship, but commerce and the professions flourished. Country estates were once again large and richly productive, absorbing many smaller properties, and introducing new systems, such as Townshend's four-course rotation of crops in 1730.

An urge towards charitable benevolence, begun chiefly among the dissident sects, was a marked feature of the age. Philosophic writing by sceptics and agnostics brought in a wave of new and politically untrammelled thought.

The highways were improved by the setting-up of toll-gates, compelling users of the roads to pay towards their upkeep. The stage-coach, introduced by mid-century, was drawn by two or four horses and could carry six passengers inside. Private carriages were lighter and more elegant. This was the age of highwaymen. On country roads that were still unmetalled wheeled traffic was at some times of the year unusable, and the best way of getting about was on horseback. Women often rode pillion behind their menfolk to church or to visit friends. Pack-horses were largely superseded by wagons and carts during this period. Water transport was also improved with the construction of aqueducts and networks of canals.

Villages no longer had to supply all the needs of a neighbourhood. Market and manufacturing towns now had a variety of shops, selling goods of all kinds from abroad as well as home products.

Jewish financiers came to England from Holland, and established themselves as stockbrokers and bankers. The Quakers also entered financial affairs, and founded county and provincial banks.

A standing Army had been formed gradually during the seventeenth century, so that regular forces took part in the campaign against France under Marlborough in the early years of the eighteenth.

Soldiers and sailors were mercilessly flogged, and punished in other severe ways, for even the smallest offence. Soldiers had no barracks, but were billeted in alehouses, where they were unwelcome. Their duties included the putting down of riots and smuggling. In the Navy, the pay was poor, the food bad, and the punishment and discipline as harsh as in the Army. The press-gang recruited men by force as the only means of keeping the numbers high.

In 1776, the thirteen states of America, after many disputes, seceded from England, and the ensuing War of Independence resulted in England's loss of her American colonies.

There were now theatres in most large provincial towns, and companies of strolling players played in barns and town halls. There was a dearth of good new plays in the middle of the century, but old dramas and comedies were continually revived, and Shakespeare was played in strangely distorted versions. In the 1770s, Goldsmith and Sheridan wrote their famous comedies. Opera and ballet were popular on the London stage. Literacy increased throughout the kingdom. Book-publishing was carried on in provincial towns as well as in London. Circulating libraries existed in London and provincial centres from 1740.

There was a form of tax for newspapers—the Government stamp, which began at a halfpenny for two sheets and a penny for four, increasing to fourpence between 1712 and 1815.

The newspapers contained reports on foreign affairs, general articles, poetry, correspondence and many advertisements. After 1771, reports of political debates were included.

Among country dwellers the daughters of the parson and the squire might share a governess with girls from other houses. Tutors were often descendants of the French refugees of the 1680s. The chance of a good education seems to have been better at home, as far as the upper classes were concerned, as the standard of boys' schools was variable. The English universities were very lax, run by clerics and conducting few examinations. Cottagers' children went to the small village schools organised by individual schoolmasters and the 'dame' schools run by women who had often had little education themselves. Schooling for both sexes at this level did not replace other tasks, such as spinning wool in their homes from the age of four years, and minding sheep or helping with land-clearance and field-labour as soon as they were old enough. Many children never learned to read, write, or understand figures. Early in the century, however, dissenting sects whose members were debarred by law from the universities, and by law or custom from many schools, opened schools of their own, giving excellent education at a moderate cost. The Anglican Church in turn opened charity schools in towns, cities and villages to give education to the poor.

In 1745, the Foundling Hospital was opened in London, and 'parish infants' were admitted. Entry was limited, however, and many babies died in the workhouses where they were born and abandoned.

Prison reform was another interest of the charitable. The prisons were filthy and crowded, prisoners of all ages and both sexes, including children, being herded together indiscriminately. At the end of the century, there were two hundred crimes punishable by hanging. These included stealing goods from a shop to the value of five shillings, or anything from the person, however trivial the object. Sheep-stealing, horse-stealing and coining were also crimes for which a man or woman might be hanged. Whipping was a punishment often carried out in the street.

With the advance of medical science new hospitals were founded, notably Guy's in London, 1725, and Manchester Royal Infirmary, 1752. On the Continent, however, monasteries and convents still carried much of the burden of education and hospital care.

COSTUME OF THE PERIOD: 1715–1780

Hair—Men: The natural hair of working-men and artisans was cut in a thick 'bobbed' fashion and brought forward over the forehead. Servants, sedan-chairmen, hairdressers and men of similar standing often grew it to about shoulder-length and tied it back with a narrow black ribbon. It could be plaited into a queue. A curl or roll of hair (sometimes two) was formed above the ears, and sometimes a 'scratch-wig' or front-piece was worn and mingled with the natural hair.

The 'bob' wig, usually grey, was worn by elderly men, lawyers, doctors and others of professional standing, also servants of senior status. It was taken back from the brow or parted in the centre, and could end at collar-level or fall to the shoulders. A brown version of this was worn by tradesmen of good position and upper servants. In this case it was full at the back and sides and ended at the collar. The full-bottomed wig in brown or grey was worn by magistrates and legal and civic dignitaries. Ecclesiastics wore it in grey.

Hair—Women: At the beginning of the period a small coiffure was coming into fashion for all classes. The hair was taken back from the brow, sometimes with a centre-parting, and put up in a knot near the top of the head or flattened in swathes across the back. When the fashion for a pompadour front came in, about mid-century, the version worn by middle-class and working women was moderate in size. Powdered hair and wigs were not much worn by these women.

Headdress—Men: The tricorne hat in various forms was worn by men of all classes throughout the period. The 'night-cap', a soft cap with a close-fitting brim turned up all round, was worn by gentry at home in place of the wig, and by artisans and labourers over the hair while at work. It could also be made in the shape of a loosely draped beret without a turn-up. The round felt hat with a pliable brim, which had been in use intermittently for centuries, was worn by elderly men, those of conservative tastes, artisans, labourers and farm-workers.

Headdress—Women: The pinner, a flat round cap of white lawn or muslin, edged with lace or embroidery, was worn over the upswept hair and continued until the 1780s. It could have long streamers at the back. A head-fitting cap with lappets at sides and back was frequently worn with the lappets pinned up on the head. The 'round-eared' cap had superseded this by about 1730. It fitted the head and was turned back in front with some width at the sides, or had an embroidered or lace-edged frill coming forward in front. Its plain or narrowly frilled back was tied in with draw-strings. A head-fitting bonnet-shaped cap that could be fastened under the chin was worn from the 1720s to '50s. Mob-caps were small, low-crowned and perched on the head, resembling the pinner until the 1760s when they were a little larger but still flat, and set back to leave room for the raised front of the coiffure. A mixture of the mob and the round-eared cap known as the *dormeuse*, but larger and with a higher crown, fitted over the larger style of hairdressing and was worn from the 1750s to the '80s.

A hood with shoulder-cape, usually of white linen, was worn by working women, particularly the elderly. The hats worn by working or middle-class women were usually of the *bergère* type, tied on over an under-cap, with a wide brim and shallow crown. The hat tilted forward and turned up at the back in the late 1770s and the '80s was worn by all classes.

Garments—Men: The long-waisted coat with a flare low down on the skirt was giving way at the beginning of this period to the coat with a normal waistline and widely flared skirt. The flare was moderate in workaday dress and the cuffs of ordinary size. The skirts of the coat had less flare in the '50s and '60s, and by 1770 were narrow, falling away from a fastening at the chest to narrow tails. There was now a standing turned-over collar.

A plain linen neckcloth was worn throughout with working dress. The waistcoat had sleeves in the first part of the period, and in this form survived mid-century as an indoor jacket frequently worn by servants. It varied in length to suit the coat, ending as a rule at the hips. A coat with a flat round collar was known as a frock. It was originally a working-man's garment, also worn informally by the gentry from 1730.

In working dress stockings were covered by the knee-breeches, not rolled outside them.

Long greatcoats with cape collars extending to the shoulders or with flat round collars were worn throughout the period. Smocks were worn by farm-labourers.

Garments—Women: The basis of women's workaday dress was the close-fitting boned bodice and the full skirt, worn over petticoats and clearing the ground. The outer skirt was often bunched up, showing the petticoat. The top of the chemise showed at the edge of the bodice. Stockings were kept up by garters. Aprons were almost always worn.

Sleeves at the outset of the period had turned-back cuffs at the elbow, showing the ends of the chemise sleeves; alternatively a corset-bodice was worn with petticoats, and the top of the chemise, with rolled-up sleeves, formed the bodice. A narrow frill took the place of the elbow-cuff about 1740. The fichu, tucked in at the bosom, was worn from about 1730, varied by a square of woollen or cotton stuff folded into a triangle crossed over and tied in front or at the back.

In the '40s and '50s the ends of the fichu could hang down in front, caught loosely together on the bosom by narrow ribbons attached to the bodice.

Most practical dresses were closed in front, but in the '60s and '70s more were open. The long cloaks worn for travelling had hoods attached in Red-Riding-Hood style.

Footwear—Men: For ordinary purposes men wore flat-soled black leather shoes, with buckles and long vamps until the '70s, when vamps were lower and a small ornament replaced the buckle. Stout riding-boots or thick-soled shoes with gaiters were worn by farm-workers.

Footwear—Women: Shoes of black or coloured leather or fabric with small heels and long buckled vamps were worn. Stockings were in scarlet, sky-blue, cherry-colour, green, grey, black and white.

Materials, Colours and Ornament: Wool, homespun, mohair, frieze, cloth, broadcloth, corduroy, twill, fustian velvet and linsey-woolsey were used for practical clothes, with linen and cotton for men's shirts and the same for women's thinner dresses, which were also made of cambric, chintz, calico, muslin and lawn. Colours for men were subdued, and included dull blue and green, brown, snuff-colour, grey, mole, dark claret and black. Women wore bright pale colours, with small checks and flower-patterns and occasionally stripes.

Ornament was usually confined to buttons, ribbon-bows and rosettes.

151. Tailor. 1720

Hair: The hair is of shoulder-length, slightly curled and allowed to hang loosely.

Headdress: The 'night-cap', worn as a working cap, has a black velvet upturned brim and a crown of segmented pieces of material in black, green and yellow. There is a button or small ornament on the top.

Garments: The tailor wears a sleeved waistcoat of green poplin with black buttons, and a yellow neckcloth. His breeches are of black cloth.

Stockings: These are of good-quality yellow cotton and are rolled at the knees, the left one having slipped down a little as the man sits on a table with one knee crossed over the other.

Shoes: Green leather flat-soled mules are worn.

Accessories: The tailor is stitching a man's coat that he is repairing.

152. Vagrant or Poor Peasant. About 1728

Hair: This is long and straggling, lying on the shoulders.

Headdress: A small battered hat in black felt is worn at an angle.

Garments: The man wears a shabby grey coat with a pocket low down on its slightly flared skirt. The large turned-back cuff is missing.

Hose: The man has on leather leggings, of a neutral colour indeterminate through wear, with a webbing band under the instep.

Shoes: He wears old and worn flat-soled shoes.

Accessories: He carries a wooden staff.

153. Maid-Servant. About 1730

Hair: The hair is taken up to a small chignon on the top of the head, hidden by the cap.

Headdress: The white linen 'round-eared' cap has a frill framing the face. It is short at the back.

Garments: The long-waisted close-fitting bodice is laced down the back. The neckline is wide and the full sleeves are three-quarter length, sewn into bands at the ends. The skirt is only moderately full and ends above the shoes. The gown is of calico with pink stripes on a pale lavender-blue ground. A white apron is worn.

Shoes: The shoes are of blue fabric tied with pink ribbon, and have raised heels.

Accessories: The girl is carrying a pottery or pewter jug in one hand and a plate of food, held with a cloth, in the other. A black ribbon is worn round the neck, tied at the back.

154. Manservant. 1730s

Hair: The natural hair, or a 'bob-wig', is taken back from the brow and arranged in short curls at the sides and back.

Garments: The calf-length old-fashioned coat is of a snuff-brown cloth, worn over a long plain buff-coloured waist-coat. The pockets of the coat are at a low level, and the plain, rather full wide sleeves have fairly large turned-back cuffs. A crossed-over cravat of white linen is worn. The knee-breeches are unseen beneath the waistcoat.

Stockings: These are of white cotton.

Shoes: The flat-soled shoes have buckles and short tongues.

Accessories: The servant is polishing a drinking-glass with a cloth.

155. Maid-Servant or Villager with Pottery Bowl. 1740

Hair: Only a little of the hair over the forehead can be seen.

Headdress: The bonnet-shaped cap of white linen has a double frill surrounding the face and wide side-lappets which in this case have been pinned up over the head.

Garments: The bodice is of pale blue-green twill, with a very deep basque which turns it into a kind of jacket. It has white turned-up cuffs to the three-quarter sleeves. A triangular white cotton kerchief is worn round the neck and tucked into the front fastening of the bodice. The skirt, ending just below the ankles, is striped in orange, brown and black. The girl has put a length of sacking over her white apron to protect it.

Stockings: These are of light fawn-coloured cotton.

Shoes: The low-heeled shoes of brown leather have tongues, and straps across the insteps.

Accessories: The girl is carrying a brown pottery bowl.

156. Maid-Servant with Cup of Chocolate. 1743

Hair: This can hardly be seen under the cap.

Headdress: The head-fitting 'round-eared' cap is of white muslin lined with pink silk, and bound with a narrow black ribbon. A white frill in front is covered by another wider one of white lace.

Garments: The jacket of lime-yellow taffetas has a small bustle at the back. The sleeves are turned back just below the elbow, showing the ends of the white chemise-sleeves. A white lawn fichu is tucked into the front of the bodice. The full skirt, ending above the shoes, is of mole-coloured taffetas. The white lawn apron has a small bib fastened to the bodice.

Shoes: These are of fabric matching the colour of the skirt, and are tied with lime-yellow ribbons. Stitching ornaments the vamps of the shoes.

Accessories: The maid is carrying a cup of chocolate on a small tray.

157. Man-Servant. About 1750

Hair: The wig is brown, rounded in shape and covering the ears.

Garments: The coat is of thick cloth in brick-red, with large buttons and buttoned flap-pockets at the sides. It has a plain neckline, large turned-back cuffs and a widely flared skirt. Dark-brown knee-breeches and a buff-yellow waistcoat are worn. The linen neckcloth is parchment-coloured.

Stockings: The stockings are of good-quality cream-coloured cotton.

Shoes: The buckled shoes are of black leather.

Accessories: The man carries a tray with a coffee-pot and two small handle-less cups with saucers.

158. Lady's Maid. 1750s

Hair: This is hardly seen under the cap, but is actually taken back in a moderate-sized roll from the forehead, with a flattened chignon fitting into the cap at the back.

Headdress: The cap of white lawn fits the head and has three folds laid across the front, one on top of another, with a single one behind them, giving a fashionably wide appearance.

Garments: The gown of lime-green taffetas is worn over a wide oval hoop, giving considerable width over the hips and comparative flatness in the front, while there is some fullness at the back. The neckline is square, with a narrow edging of ivory-coloured gauze. The base of the bodice is pointed and its front is open, showing softly ruffled horizontal rows of the gauze over a silk foundation of the same colour. The sleeves end at the elbow in several matching rows of pleated ruffles. An apron of parchment-coloured muslin is worn.

Shoes: These are covered in blue ribbed silk and have small raised heels.

Accessories: The girl wears a blue ribbon round her throat and is examining a rose-coloured gauze scarf, trimmed with gold fringe and gold tissue flowers, belonging to her mistress.

159. American Housewife. 1760

Hair: A little of this is seen over the forehead and at the sides.

Headdress: A head-fitting cap of white lawn has a frill framing the face and is tied on under the chin.

Garments: The gown is of grey poplin with sleeves turned back at the elbows, showing the white frilled chemise-sleeves. The full skirt reaches the ground. A voluminous white lawn fichu, a white apron and transparent black mittens are worn.

Footwear: The tip of one black kid slipper can be seen.

Accessories: The housewife is holding a cup and saucer.

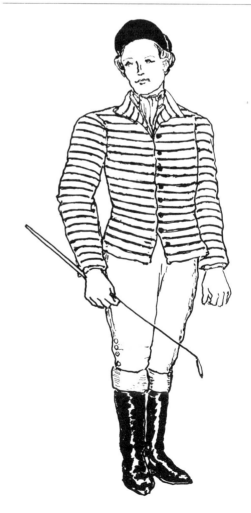

160. Groom in a Gentleman's Service. 1760

Hair: The hair, which is kept rather short and unplentiful, is rolled upward a little at the sides above the ears and is taken back into a small narrow queue (unseen).

Headdress: The black peaked cap resembles that of a jockey today.

Garments: The 'jump' jacket has horizontal stripes of green on a white ground. It has a turned-down collar and is worn fastened down the front. The breeches are of light-fawn buckskin. The plain neckcloth is of white linen.

Boots: These are black leather riding-boots with tan leather tops.

Accessories: The groom carries a riding-crop.

161. French Milkmaid. 1760s

Hair: This is taken back from the forehead in a roll.

Headdress: The white linen cap is turned back in front and fits the head at the back.

Garments: The girl wears a jacket-bodice with a deep basque in blue glazed cotton. It is open, showing the corset laced over the chemise. It has shoulder-pieces in place of sleeves and the elbow-length puffed sleeves of the chemise are seen. The blue glazed cotton skirt is bunched up all round, showing a dark rose-coloured linen under-skirt ornamented with narrow black bands near the hem. A white apron is tied on over the blue skirt but under the jacket-bodice.

Stockings: The stockings are of white cotton.

Shoes: These are of grey leather, with buckles.

Accessories: The milkmaid carries a metal container of milk on her head.

162. Maidservant or Villager. 1760s

Hair: Only the roll of hair over the forehead is seen.

Headdress: A mob-cap of moderate size is set back on the head.

Garments: The gown is of soft blue glazed linen. It has a fitted bodice with a low square neckline and sleeves turned back, with white cuffs just below the elbows. The bell-shaped skirt ends just above the shoes. A plain white apron is worn.

Footwear: The shoes are of blue fabric, with small bows tied over the instep and slightly raised heels.

Accessories: The girl carries a flat wooden tray with an edge of basket-work and some roses laid upon it.

163. French Peasant Youth. 1760–70

Hair: The hair is cut to a short 'bobbed' length and is not much seen beneath the hat.

Hat: The hat is of dark-brown felt, turned up all round and bound in biscuit-colour. A small ornament of this ribbon-binding decorates a depression in the hat-brim.

Garments: The loose open jacket and knee-breeches are of a lighter brown than the hat. The jacket has small shoulder-capes in place of sleeves and the waistcoat-sleeves are seen. A wide neckcloth is tied loosely in a bow in front.

Stockings: The wrinkled stockings are of light biscuit-coloured yarn.

Shoes: These are of natural reversed calf, with short tongues and ties over the insteps.

164. Lady's Maid. 1760–70

Hair: The hair is rolled back from the forehead and shows a little in front. The base of the chignon and some short pendent curls can be seen at the back.

Headdress: The maid is wearing a modified version of the cap known as a *dormeuse*. It is of ivory-coloured silk muslin and has a length of lilac-pink ribbon laid across it. The frilled edging comes forward on each side in a curve from a central point above the forehead, hiding the temples and diminishing towards the back. The cap itself lies comparatively flatly on the head, without the usual size and depth of the *dormeuse*.

Garments: The over-dress is of lavender-blue silk with a fitted bodice, sleeves with deep ruffles of ivory silk muslin and a Watteau pleat at the back, devolving into a bunched-up skirt. This exposes part of the silk underskirt in lavender-blue and pink silk stripes.

Stockings: These are of cream-coloured silk.

Shoes: The shoes, covered in lavender-blue ribbed silk, have raised heels.

Accessories: The maid is carrying a jar of cosmetic and her mistress's fan.

165. Journeyman-Craftsman. 1770s

Hair: The natural hair is worn fairly long and curls in at the ends.

Headdress: The man carries his tricorne hat under his arm.

Garments: The blue-green coat is old and shabby, with unfashionable fullness in the skirt. The left sleeve is patched and the large turned-back cuffs have been removed, probably to facilitate work and to be able to keep the coat on under cold outdoor conditions. The blue breeches are hardly seen. Fawn-coloured cloth gaiters are worn as a protection against the weather. The neckcloth is of white linen.

Shoes: Shabby brown-coloured leather shoes are worn.

Accessories: The man is presenting a bill for work done to an employer. He is a jobbing craftsman, employed in such work as mending window-frames, doors and furniture, painting walls and sometimes inn-signs or other notices. Such men would go about the country, taking the stage-coach from their own town or village and walking long distances from a convenient stop to a farm or other place of employment.

166. Welsh Country Woman. 1770s

Hair: This is hardly seen under the cap.

Headdress: A frilled white lawn head-fitting cap is worn. Over it is a black felt hat with a round flat brim, a crown flat on the top and a narrow band of ribbon with two ends hanging from it at the back. The hat is set well back on the head.

Garments: The bodice is of the waistcoat shape, short and fitted to the figure, with long plain sleeves. It is of dark-green velveteen and ends at the hips. The overskirt of grey-green woollen stuff is bunched up to show an underskirt striped in red and grey.

Stockings: These are of grey wool.

Shoes: The black leather shoes have flat heels.

Accessories: The woman carries a short walking-staff.

167. Welsh Farm-Worker. 1770s

Hair: The hair is taken back from the face and worn fairly long.

Headdress: The dark-brown felt hat has its brim turned up at the back.

Garments: The loose 'jump' jacket is of blue and red-brown frieze mixture. The knee-breeches are of brown woollen fabric, unfastened at the knees.

Stockings: Wrinkled light-brown woollen stockings are worn.

Shoes: The buckled shoes are of brown leather.

Accessories: The labourer is holding a turving-spade.

168. French Foster-Nurse and Child. 1770s

Hair: The hair is dressed in a roll in front, taken up from the temples, and swept up from the back into a similar roll, with combs across the top of the head to keep them in place. The baby's hair is short and curly.

Headdress: The baby wears a round blue tasselled cap.

Garments: The woman wears a waistcoat-shaped bodice with a deep flared basque of brick-red cloth. A triangular green silk kerchief is worn round the neck. The plum-red overskirt of thick glazed cotton is tucked under all round, showing an underskirt striped in plum-red and green. The baby's dress is of dotted blue and white muslin.

Stockings: The woman wears biscuit-coloured cotton stockings. The baby's are of white silk.

Shoes: The foster-nurse has on brown buckled shoes of reversed leather, with low heels. The baby's slippers are blue.

Accessories: The baby is wearing leading-strings held by the nurse.

169. French Shepherdess. 1770s

Hair: The hair is drawn up into a roll under the back part of the hat-brim, with a ringlet hanging down.

Headdress: The straw hat is tilted up at the back and worn at an angle with a band passing under the hair to keep it in place. This fashion is seen in costumes of all grades of society in England and France by women doing farm work as well as for more elegant occasions.

Garments: The jacket-bodice of greyish-green sateen is open, showing the corset laced over the white chemise. A triangular pale-yellow kerchief is worn round the neck and tucked in at the bosom. The bodice is sleeveless and the shoulder and sleeve of the chemise have slipped down over the upper arm. The sleeve ends in a band just below the elbow. The bodice has a long basque at the sides and back, laid over the bunched-up skirt. The underskirt is of heavy yellow linen. The large white apron is caught up on the left side.

Stockings: These are of green cotton.

Shoes: The buckled shoes are of black leather with small raised heels.

Accessories: The shepherdess carries a light staff, to which she has tied a flower, in her left hand, and a triangular basket of flowers in her right.

170. Manservant with Hat and Cane. 1760–70

Hair: The hair is powdered and tied back with a black ribbon. It slopes upward and backward in front and has a rolled horizontal curl on each side.

Garments: The coat follows the new sloping-away line, but does not have the upstanding collar that later became the fashion. It is of dark-blue cloth, ornamented with silver buttons along its edge and on the pocket-flap. The cuffs are narrow and are attached at the ends of the sleeves without turning back. The plain breeches and waistcoat are of ivory-coloured faced cloth. The neck-cloth is of ivory-coloured lawn.

Stockings: These are of ivory silk.

Shoes: Flat-soled buckled shoes of black leather are worn.

Accessories: The servant is holding a tricorne hat and a cane to hand to his master or to a departing guest.

171. Ordinary Citizen. 1770s

Hair: The unpowdered hair is taken back simply from the face and tied into a small queue.

Headdress: The black felt hat has the forward peak of the tricorne, but is turned up across the back.

Garments: The man is wearing a 'frock' of dark-green cloth. It has a flat turned-down collar and a skirt full from the hips with inconspicuous vertically placed pockets. The sleeves are plain and buttoned above the wrists on the outside. The breeches and waistcoat are not seen.

Stockings: The stockings are of fine grey wool.

Shoes: The buckled shoes are of black leather.

Accessories: The man carries a walking-stick.

172. Elderly French Farmer. 1770s

Hair: The old man's sparse grey hair is long enough to reach his collar, where it curls in slightly.

Headdress: His round hat of brown felt is trimmed with a wide band and has a moderate-sized brim.

Garments: The farmer wears a heavy greatcoat of russet-coloured cloth, with a wide collar fastened in front. The long cuffs have been removed. His waistcoat and jacket are hidden by the greatcoat, which has a few button-and-loop fastenings. His breeches are of brown leather, ending above the knees and fastened with buttons on the outside of the legs. His coarse leggings of natural wool are rolled above the knees, probably supported by garters beneath the folds at the top or below the knees.

Boots: He wears heavy countryman's boots ending below the knees.

Accessories: He carries a stick.

173. American Citizen Dressed in the Quaker Tradition. Late 18th Century

Hair: The straight hair is worn at shoulder-length.

Headdress: The black felt hat is turned up in front and down at the back. There is a depression in the centre front of the large brim.

Garments: The coat, waistcoat and knee-breeches are all of dove-grey cloth. The buttons are covered in the same stuff. A plain white neckcloth is worn.

Stockings: The stockings are of dove-grey wool.

Shoes: The black leather shoes have high vamps but no buckles.

Accessories: The man carries a walking-stick.

174. Town Crier. Late Eighteenth Century

Hair: A powdered wig with curls rolled at the sides is worn.

Headdress: The large black felt tricorne is edged with two rows of gold braid. It is worn set back on the head and the central point is high, in the fashion of the 1760s.

Garments: The long coat of dark-blue cloth, lined with scarlet, has only moderate width in the skirt. It has brass buttons but only artificial buttonholes, as it is not intended to fasten. Brass buttons also decorate the cuffs. The wide collar is scarlet, edged with gold braid. The waistcoat is also scarlet and the knee-breeches dark blue. A plain white neckcloth is worn.

Stockings: These are of white cotton.

Shoes: Black buckled shoes are worn.

Accessories: The crier carries a handbell to attract attention for the news and announcements he gives out.

175. Maid-Servant with Frying-Pan. 1780s

Hair: Only the roll of hair over the forehead is seen.

Headdress: A dark-green kerchief is tied in a top-knot over the white mob-cap, the frills of which can be seen at the sides and over the forehead.

Garments: The dress of pale-green and yellow stripes is of linen. It is sleeveless and ends just above the ground. The long white linen chemise-sleeves are visible. The large bib of the twill apron, of light cinnamon-brown with narrow vermilion stripes, covers the corset-bodice of the dress in front. A plain white fichu is worn.

Shoes: Only the tip of one brown fabric shoe is seen.

Accessories: The girl is holding an iron frying-pan with a long curved handle.

CHAPTER EIGHT
1780–1850

Advances in agricultural methods in this period were made possible by large commercial profits. New fertilisers and the use of new inventions brought further capital into farming, and the rapid developments brought about agricultural revolution. Waste land and wooded ground had been cleared, and hedged fields enclosed to be used in rotation for pasture and crops. Landless labourers were employed by leasehold farming tenants, and women worked on the land all the year round, instead of seasonally.

Many former rural workers went into the wool and cotton industries in the towns. But work for reasonable pay under fair conditions was not to last. Inventions that developed more quickly than man's adaptation to their use resulted in a restless unsettled attitude towards work and strife between employer and employee. Hurried building for the sake of commercial utility produced streets of small mean houses, which still form the pattern of some industrial towns.

Trade difficulties during the French Revolutionary and Napoleonic Wars because of blockades and the opening and closing of European markets frequently led to unemployment. After the peace of 1815, post-war retrenchments by other nations, and consequent smaller demand for goods, brought down prices and wages. Many commercial enterprises which had stored up produce in the hope of selling it at pre-war prices, or more, failed altogether, and for many poverty and unemployment ensued. From time to time, rioting broke out, resulting in bloodshed and the destruction of machinery and burning of property by workers who blamed the new mechanisation for many of their troubles.

Cottage industries collapsed, and families were split up to move into factory work at low wages. Children from the age of five years were taken away in cartloads by the local authorities to be apprenticed to industrialists. They stood at their work for twelve to thirteen hours a day and were starved and beaten into submission.

In 1795, the Poor Law was amended so that every labourer, whether able to work or not, was entitled to relief according to the number of his children, legitimate or otherwise, from the funds of the parish in which he lived. Those who paid the Poor Rate were faced with enormous expense and the farmers reduced wages to a pittance. The number of children born in or out of wedlock naturally increased, and parish authorities used every means to reduce the rural populations, even forcible removal of adults and children regardless of family ties. Cottages were pulled down and land taken out of cultivation in order to drive people away, but they were equally unwelcome elsewhere.

After the Napoleonic Wars, however, programmes of reform were set in motion. The Emancipation Act, 1829, enabled Catholics to vote, take office, sit in Parliament and serve as officers in the Army. In 1833, the slave trade was abolished. The number of crimes involving the death-penalty was reduced.

By 1833, factory regulations laid down that no-one under eighteen was to work for more than ten hours a day, children under thirteen not more than eight and those over thirteen and under eighteen not more than twelve hours or sixty-nine in one week. Workhouses were built and parish relief denied to any able-bodied man. Mothers of illegitimate children must support them, but by an Act of 1844, a woman could demand the maintenance of an illegitimate child from its father. After five years' residence in a parish, members of a family could not be forcibly separated and sent away, and destitute people might be given shelter without reference to the parish in which they had lived. In the second quarter of the century, large numbers of emigrants sailed to the Colonies under organised schemes.

Country people who removed to cities and towns often regretted the loss of their still unspoilt and beautiful rural surroundings. Paintings of the late eighteenth and early nineteenth centuries show us a countryside of great beauty, and some prosperity, in districts where mechanisation and rebuilding were slow to encroach, or which escaped them altogether. The way of life of great houses and their attached farms had continued throughout the vicissitudes in which the poorer labourers had become involved. Marriages and changes of tenancy had bridged the gulf between the yeoman class and the minor aristocracy, so that families of mixed origin often presented the character of simple and countrified people.

The textile and other industries benefited by new inventions such as the 'flying shuttle', which speeded up the process of weaving, and the 'spinning-jenny', whereby one man could spin six threads at once. Steam power, destined to supersede water-power, was introduced with the development of Watt's steam engine. In agriculture, a threshing-machine, worked at first by horses and later by steam, a seed-drill widely used by farmers from 1800, and from America a mechanical reaper drawn by horses were among the agricultural improvements in use by mid-century. Many other inventions affected domestic life: methods of canning food between 1809 and 1830, a form of sewing-machine also about 1830, improved flush water-closets, gas lighting, at first in streets and then for homes and public buildings.

Advances had been made in medicine that effectually reduced the death-rate. Jenner's discovery of the vaccine inoculation against smallpox took place at the end of the eighteenth century, and the invention of a form of stethoscope in the early nineteenth. James Young Simpson introduced the first use of chloroform for general anaesthesia in the 1840s.

By 1814, George Stephenson had constructed a steam locomotive. The first goods-carrying railway train ran between Stockton and Darlington in 1825. Lines were soon built between other towns. Within another ten years, networks of railways existed in most European countries.

The first half of the century saw the rapid development of the application of steam power. Fundamental discoveries in the field of electricity were the basis of a new source of power for industry and domestic use that flourished in the second half of the century. The Cunard and the P. & O. Companies were formed in 1840. By the end of the next decade, travel by steamship was possible to all continents.

COSTUME OF THE PERIOD: 1780–1850

Hair and Wigs—Men: The use of the natural hair was increasing. It was usually tied in a short queue or worn in a 'bobbed' shape. The queue was worn by tradesmen, clerks and other functionaries until about 1810, some servants wearing it into the '20s and '30s.

They also wore the 'bob' wig and its longer counterpart until about 1810. Footmen wore hair-powder or a grey or white *perruque* or *toupet*. During the 1790s men's natural hair was thick and loosely arranged. In the early nineteenth century it was cut short at the back and brought forward from the crown of the head. A side or centre parting was usual from the 1820s onwards, when curls and waves were worn. A parting extending from the forehead to the base of the skull could be worn from the 1840s.

In the 1780s and '90s most men were clean-shaven. Side-burns were worn early in the nineteenth century. From the end of the 1820s a fringe chin-beard joining the longer side-whiskers could be worn. A small moustache was optional with this from 1811; a lip-tuft could be worn with the moustache. Whiskers and moustaches had increased in size by mid-century; an Imperial or goatee beard could be worn from about 1830.

Hair—Women: Women wore their hair in a pompadour, usually unpowdered, in the 1780s. Their hair was shorter from about 1795 and showed less under the cap. A chignon, low, high or at mid-level, with curls over the forehead and sometimes over the head, was worn in the early 1800s.

By 1820 the chignon was near or on the top of the head, with a centre-parting and a wider shape at the sides. In the middle '30s smooth pomaded hair was dressed with a few ringlets, with the chignon at the crown or top of the head. In the '40s the chignon was low or at mid-level.

Headdress—Men: The tricorne was generally turned up across the back of the head, and soft pliable caps of differing types were worn by working-men. The round felt hat was in use by all classes until mid-century. A tall-crowned, flat-topped felt hat was also worn in the 1780s and '90s.

The top-hat of moderate height and the hard-crowned hat worn from 1800 onwards were evolved from this.

Headdress—Women: Hats were perched up in the 1780s and in utilitarian dress were simply trimmed. A large mob-cap was worn in the '80s and '90s. From the later '90s onwards head-fitting bonnets and plain brimmed hats, some set back on the head, were adapted to working clothes, as was the variety of caps, brimmed hats and large bonnets of the late 1820s and '30s. In the '40s bonnets with closer brims were the main item of head-gear for all women.

Garments—Men: Coats were nearly all of cloth or other woollen stuff. A coat square-cut at the waist, with tails, dating from about 1790, the sloping-away coat and the 'frock', now double-breasted with lapels, were the main items until the single- or double-breasted frock-coat appeared about 1816.

Pantaloons and breeches (out of fashion by the '40s), went with the darker coats. Peg-top trousers, strapped under the instep, came in about 1820. Sleeves were usually full at the shoulders, tapering to the wrists.

The stock was worn from the later 1790s, though the cravat was in use for many more years, and a starched white collar with points upturned on to the cheeks, from about 1800.

Waistcoats still had sleeves for wear by working people. They were generally double-breasted from the '90s with a small standing collar and lapels, and became jackets worn by men in numerous occupations.

Men wore caped or plain greatcoats or cloaks in the early years, the two latter items being in use throughout the period. From about 1820 the frock-coat was usually worn without a greatcoat. It had a high collar and broad lapels. It was made at first in one figure-fitting piece, but its skirt was attached at the waist from 1830 and it hung more loosely.

Garments—Women: The 'round' dress, with fullness at the back, was worn with a *bouffant* fichu or a neckerchief in the '80s and early '90s. This could have long close-fitting or three-quarter sleeves. In the mid-'90s the uncorseted high-waisted dress had puffed sleeves, often with long close sleeves added. Decorative collars and ruffs were worn in the 1820s. The waist was lower by 1825 and normal by 1827. Bodices were tightly corseted again. Leg-of-mutton sleeves tapered from shoulder to wrist. The shoulder-line was very wide, with broad flat collars.

The skirt was immensely full at the hem. About 1835 the upper sleeve drooped down-wards. By 1840 many sleeves were long and plain. Round flat collars fastened at the throat. The bodice was long-waisted and the skirt bell-shaped.

Outer wraps followed the form of the dress. Loose mantles and shaped wraps went with the 'round' dress. Cloaks, shaped stoles and 'pelisses' accompanied the high-waisted dresses, and wide-shouldered tight-waisted coats the ensuing fashions. Close-fitting hip-length jackets and three-quarter length mantles covered the dress of the 1840s.

Shoes—Men: Shoes had flat, thin soles with shallow heels, optionally trimmed with bows or flat buckles. They could be worn by indoor servants.

Boots—Men: Boots ending just below the knee were worn early in the period. For service-able wear they had flat heels. Bootees, sometimes with cloth uppers, were worn from about 1818, covered by the trousers from 1820 or so, and with elastic side-gussets from 1847. Gaiters were added to heavy boots by agricultural workers.

Shoes—Women: Women's shoes had high vamps and buckles, with raised heels, early in the period. By 1800 their slippers had thin flat soles. About 1840 small heels were added.

Boots—Women: Bootees buttoning in front were worn from about 1815. They could have elastic side-gussets or laces on the inside from 1847.

Materials, Colour and Ornament: Cloth, homespun and other woollen fabrics were used for men's coats, with stockinette for pantaloons. Trousers and waistcoats could be plain, checked, striped or variously patterned, and were lighter than the dark- or neutral-coloured coats.

Women's serviceable gowns were in pale, deep or neutral colours, made of woollen stuffs and in plain, printed, checked or striped cotton, linen or other thin material.

Business and professional men wore watches on fobs, and after 1830 watches on chains, cuff-links and studs. Women, when they wore jewellery with working dress, had lockets or brooches to fasten their collars from the late 1820s.

176. French Farm-Labourer. 1780s

Hair: The hair hangs raggedly from the back of the cap.

Headdress: The peak of the dark-red Phrygian cap has fallen backward rather than forward.

Garments: The short close-fitting 'jump' jacket or sleeved waistcoat of tan-coloured woollen or linen stuff is of a type already worn throughout most of the century by working-men. The knee-breeches are of the same colour, buttoned on the outside of the knee.

Hose: Brown leather leggings are suspended by tabs from the legs of the breeches. The man wears no stockings.

Footwear: His feet are bare.

Accessories: The labourer is wielding a three-pronged metal fork.

177. French Advocate. 1783

Hair: The hair of the grey-white wig is drawn back and upward from the forehead. It is rolled over the ears and round the back of the head. The long tail of hair at the back is doubled at the bottom and knotted into its own length.

Headdress: A black conical hat with a small ornament on the top is carried in the hand.

Garments: The black gown has very wide sleeves and trails on the ground at the back. It fastens with buttons down the front. A white lawn neckcloth is worn and a wrist-frill of the shirt can be seen. In this case the coat is black and the end of the sleeve is visible.

Footwear: Black buckled shoes are worn.

178. Country Girl Coming from Market. 1786

Hair: The hair is loosely arranged and rather unkempt.

Headdress: A white cotton frilled cap is worn with a wide-brimmed natural straw hat put on over it.

Garments: A kerchief is tucked into the wide neckline of the olive-brown jacket-bodice the girl is wearing. This has sleeves ending in turned-back elbow-cuffs. It is pulled together at the top fastening. The skirt that goes with it is turned up all round over the hips, showing its terra-cotta red lining and a torn and ragged underskirt of indeterminate washed-out neutral colours striped in maroon. Both are patched.

Stockings: These are of light-brown cotton.

Shoes: The shabby light-brown shoes are of buckskin, with low heels.

Accessories: The girl carries a basket containing asparagus and artichokes and a wicker cage containing a live hen.

179. Girl in Large Mob-Cap. 1780s–'90s

Hair: The hair is taken up in a small roll from the forehead. Only a little of it can be seen under the cap.

Headdress: The large mob-cap is unstarched and its frills hang loosely. It is tied with a black ribbon.

Garments: The dress is of yellow linen with narrow stripes of amber edged with black. It has a fitted bodice and a closed skirt bunched up at front and back. The plain sleeves are three-quarter length, fitting closely to the forearm. Part of the copper-coloured quilted sateen petticoat can be seen. A parchment-coloured kerchief is worn round the neck and tucked into the bodice. A white apron is worn.

Stockings: The stockings are of white cotton.

Shoes: The shoes of black fabric have small buckles and low, shaped heels.

180. French Revolutionary Character. 1790s

Hair: The hair is unkempt and hangs almost to the shoulders.

Headdress: The large-brimmed black felt hat is turned up in front to the left-hand side rather than in the centre, and is ornamented with a red, white and blue Revolutionary cockade.

Garments: The crumpled white cotton shirt is open at the chest and wrapped across the body without fastenings. The torn knee-breeches are of darkish-blue cloth. The shabby coat is striped in red and grey.

Hose: Thick leggings of coarse grey yarn are bound to the legs below the knees. Gaiters of darker-grey cloth, buttoned on the outside, are worn over them.

Shoes: Thick-soled clumsy black leather shoes are worn.

Accessories: The man carries a wooden club.

181. Boy Filling Street-Lamp with Oil. 1805

Hair: The hair is untidily cropped and falls forward over the forehead.

Headdress: The boy wears a battered green felt hat with a moderate-sized brim.

Garments: The short jacket is of greenish-grey frieze with knee-breeches to match. A piece of dark-red material is worn as a neckcloth over the white cotton shirt.

Stockings: These are of grey cotton.

Shoes: The shoes of black reversed calf have high vamps with small laced ties at the top.

Accessories: The boy is standing on a ladder and is pouring oil from the narrow curved spout of a jug made for the purpose into the oil-container of a street-lamp. This has a large glass globe and is attached by metal supports to a wall.

182. Dame-School Mistress. 1810

Hair: The centrally parted hair hardly shows under the cap.

Headdress: The lawn or muslin cap has a narrow frill and is tied on under the chin. It has a moderate-sized crown and is of an earlier fashion.

Garments: The mauve and white print dress has a fitted bodice and bell-shaped skirt, following the fashion of working dress in the 1760s or thereabouts. The waistline is at a normal level, with a black plush or fustian velvet shoulder-piece worn for warmth, ending just above the bosom. The sleeves end just below the elbow. A white apron is worn.

Footwear: The school mistress wears grey cotton stockings and flat-soled black fabric slippers in the style of the early nineteenth century.

Accessories: She carries a small birch.

183. Lady's Maid. About 1815.

Hair: The hair is arranged in curls over the forehead and the rest is drawn back into a chignon and small curls at the crown of the head.

Headdress: The high-crowned cap is of transparent white gauze bound with rose-pink ribbon behind the forehead-curls and again further back.

Garments: The gown of deep rose-pink ribbed silk has a high waist and ends at the ankles. The bodice is open to show a white chemise with a narrow upstanding collar, the opening filled in with folds of white muslin crossed over the bosom. The short puffed sleeves of the dress are covered with over-sleeves of the white gauze, with long sleeves to the wrist attached.

Stockings: The stockings are of white silk.

Shoes: Black fabric flat-soled slippers are worn.

Accessories: The girl is holding a letter folded in three and sealed with wax, and trying to read part of it.

184. Postman. 1820

Hair: The hair is short, but thick and curly. Small side-whiskers are worn.

Headdress: The battered black top-hat has been pushed to the back of his head.

Garments: The white shirt-frill can be seen at the opening of the buff-coloured lapelled waistcoat. The crumpled white cravat is tied in a bow in front, with the points of the collar showing on the jaws. The tail-coat, cut square at the waistline, is of claret-coloured cloth. It is double-breasted with buttons on both sides, and is worn open. The shirt-cuffs are not visible at the ends of the sleeves. The knee-breeches are of dark-green cloth.

Stockings: These are of white or off-white cotton.

Shoes: The flat-soled shoes are of black leather in the 'pump' style.

Accessories: The postman wears a small ornament as a fob at the base of his waistcoat. He carries a bag of leather and canvas to hold letters, a packet of letters in one hand and a bell in the other.

185. Gentleman's Valet. 1820

Hair: The hair is parted on the right side with a quiff arranged on the left. Some strands are brought forward over the brow and the hair at the back is dressed in a roll.

Garments: The jacket is a sleeved waistcoat of green-and-white striped sateen, with a long rolled collar of green silk. The lawn neckcloth and shirt-frill are white. The knee-breeches are of darker-green cloth. A long white apron is worn.

Stockings: These are of pearl-grey silk with embroidered clocks.

Shoes: The shallow flat-soled slippers are of black kid with black ribbon bows.

Accessories: The valet is carrying a razor and shaving-mug to shave his master.

186. Farm-Labourer Wearing a Smock. Early Nineteenth Century

Hair: The hair is straight and of a 'bobbed' length, with a casual unkempt appearance.

Headdress: The hat of rust-red felt is worn at an angle with the brim turned down.

Garments: The open collar of the white cotton shirt is seen over the wide collar of the 'holland' smock, which is buttoned down the front and has smocking on the chest and sleeves. The knee-breeches are of dark-green cloth.

Stockings: The stockings are of light-green yarn.

Boots: The short boots are made to be pulled on and are of natural leather.

Accessories: The boy is carrying a staff, and bird-scarer rattle.

187. Housewife or Maid-Servant with Taper. 1820

Hair: The hair is parted in the centre and has short ringlets at the sides. Another can be seen below the cap towards the back.

Headdress: The bonnet-shaped cap has a fairly large crown, bound with a black ribbon, and a frill surrounding the face. It is tied with streamers of its own stuff under the chin.

Garments: The high-waisted dress is of cream-coloured wool with a pattern in cherry-red. It has a starched up-standing frilled muslin collar, tied at the base of its deep V with cherry-red ribbons. The sleeves are full-length with white muslin frills at the wrists. A white lawn apron is tied on at the high waist.

Stockings: The stockings are of white silk or good-quality cotton.

Shoes: The flat-soled slippers are of soft black leather.

Accessories: The woman is lighting a candle in a tall silver candlestick with a taper.

188. American Railway Magnate. 1829

Hair: The hair is cut to look full at the back. Whiskers and a fringe beard are worn.

Headdress: The top-hat has a curved brim and is made of ivory-white plush.

Garments: The black cloth tail-coat is cut away at the waist. The sleeves fit the forearms closely and have 'goblet' cuffs. The waistcoat is of thick ivory-white taffetas. The black satin cravat has a large bow in front. The trousers are of fine ivory-white cloth, with straps under the insteps.

Boots: These are of black leather, ending unseen above the ankles.

Accessories: The magnate carries a malacca cane with a knob of ivory and gold.

189. Maid Servant. About 1830

Hair: The hair is parted in the centre and shows ringlets at the sides of the face.

Headdress: The front of the white muslin cap has ruched frills framing the face and black ribbons to tie it under the chin. The back of the cap stands up above the level of the front and covers the back of the head.

Garments: The wide white lawn collar lies flat, extending towards the shoulders. The blue check linen dress has a fitted bodice and a pyramidal skirt, very wide at the hem.

Stockings: The stockings are of thin pale-grey cotton.

Shoes: The black kid slippers have flat soles.

Accessories: The woman carries a letter on a salver.

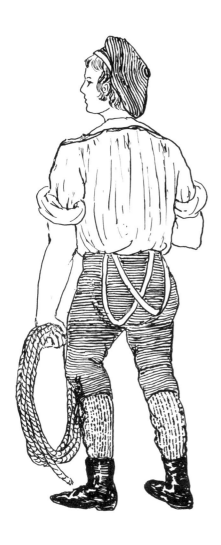

190. Ostler. 1830s

Hair: The hair is fairly long and roughly cut, with whiskers ending below the ears.

Headdress: The black beret-shaped cap is set back on the head. It has a small button in the centre of the crown.

Garments: The ostler wears a white shirt with sleeves rolled up. His braces are hanging down his back, attached to fawn whipcord riding-breeches.

Leg-Covering: He wears coarse grey woollen stockings.

Boots: His black boots end at the ankles.

Accessories: He holds a coil of rope.

191. Mail-Coach Driver. 1830s

Hair: The hair is cut short at the back. Short side-whiskers are worn.

Headdress: The driver is wearing an ivory-coloured top-hat.

Garments: The striped green-and-white sleeved waistcoat has a dark green tail-coat over it. The edges of the coat are curved over the chest and devolve into tails (unseen). The light overcoat is of parchment-coloured cloth, with close-fitting trousers to match. These are strapped under the instep. The silk cravat is green, and the white starched shirt-collar has points coming up on to the cheeks. Ivory-coloured gloves are worn.

Boots: The bootees are of fine black leather.

Accessories: The driver carries a whip.

192. Train-Driver. 1832

Hair: The hair is not seen under the cap. Side-whiskers and a fringe beard are worn.

Headdress: The dark-blue cap has a black peak and a small button on the top. It is worn at an angle, set back on the head.

Garments: The jacket is of dark-green cloth and is worn with a yellow muffler round the neck. The waistcoat and trousers are fawn-coloured.

Footwear: The driver wears black leather bootees, the tops hidden by his trousers.

193. American Hunter. 1835

Hair: The hair is long enough to lie on the shoulders.

Headdress: The hunter wears a hat of fawn-coloured felt. The crown is soft and the wide brim turned up all round. It has a tuft of feathers on the left side.

Garments: The natural leather coat is of American Indian work, with leather fringe and ornament to cover the seam below the shoulders, where the sleeve is put in, and decoration only on the seams of the sleeves. The decoration without fringe edges the pocket-flaps and is put on with fringe on the skirt of the coat. The hem of the coat, just below the knees, is stitched in leather-work. The leather trousers have long fringes on the outside of the legs.

Footwear: Leather moccasins are worn.

Accessories: The man carries a gun.

194. Maidservant with Bellows. 1835

Hair: This is not much seen beneath the cap. A ringlet hangs on each side of the face. There is a high chignon (unseen).

Headdress: A high-crowned cap of white linen with fluted edging framing the face is set well back on the head.

Garments: The gown of lilac-pink cashmere has a fitted bodice with a wide deep collar of pleated lawn finished at the centre with a dark-pink ribbon bow. It has a narrow pleated shaped frill to form an inner collar. The upper sleeves are puffed, and the lower sleeves long and close-fitting. The skirt is wide at the hem. A white embroidered apron is worn.

Stockings: These are of fine white cotton.

Shoes: The flat-soled slippers are of black kid.

195. Business Employee in Frock-Coat. About 1840

Hair: The hair is fairly thick at the back (unseen) and side-whiskers are worn.

Headdress: The tall top-hat has a narrow brim.

Garments: The black frock-coat is full-skirted and ends above the knees. It has a large rolled collar and a slightly sloping shoulder-line. The pale-yellow waistcoat has high lapels and ends just below the waist. The narrowly fitting trousers are striped in black and grey. A pale lavender-coloured cravat is tied in a bow. Clerks and shop-assistants made every effort on limited salaries to appear smart.

Footwear: Black bootees are worn, the tops hidden by the trousers.

Accessories: The man wears lavender gloves and carries a cane.

196. Woman in Large Shawl. 1840s

Hair: The hair is parted in the centre under the large bonnet-brim and put up in a chignon (unseen).

Headdress: The bonnet of fine straw has its brim turned back from the face. Behind it is a tall diminishing crown that encloses the chignon.

Garments: The fitted bodice of the black dress ends at a low level and is worn with a bell-shaped skirt. The flat-lying collar is of white linen. The sleeves are long and plain. A white apron is worn. A large fringed shawl of deep-red cashmere forms an outer wrap.

Footwear: Part of the black leather shoes can be seen.

Accessories: The woman is carrying a basket of eggs.

197. Girl and Small Boy. 1840s

Hair: The girl, aged about fourteen, has her hair put up in a loose untidy knot with a fringe in front. The boy's longish hair, also with a fringe, is unkempt.

Garments: The girl wears a tattered silk dress off the shoulders and with torn puffed sleeves, salvaged from among discarded clothes. The boy has on a ragged white cotton shirt and patched and torn blue trousers.

Stockings: The girl has on once-white stockings and the boy has none.

Shoes: Both wear thin flat-soled slippers; the girl's are black fabric and the boy's, which are split at the toes, red leather.

198. Railway Guard. About 1845

Hair: The hair is rather long and is curled in front of the ears.

Headdress: The black peaked cap has a small button on the top. It is worn at an angle, set back on the head.

Garments: The bottle-green cloth coat has a flared skirt ending at the knees and large pockets. It is double-breasted and has silver badges on both sides of the rolled lapelled collar. The sleeves diminish from the slightly high shoulders to the wrists. The trousers are of dark-grey worsted, strapped under the foot. The collar has points coming up on to the cheeks and the wide cravat is of black silk.

Footwear: Black leather bootees are worn, the tops hidden by the trousers.

Accessories: A wide black leather strap is slung from the right shoulder to the left hip. It has a silver buckle mounted with a large railway badge, and a pouch at the lower end for carrying money and valuables. The guard is holding a notebook and pencil.

199. Country Woman. About 1850

Hair: The hair is worn parted in the centre and smoothly arranged. It hardly shows under the cap.

Headdress: The white linen bonnet-like cap has a frill in front which frames the face, a wide band of linen behind it and the part covering the back of the head gathered on to it.

Garments: The dress is of dove-coloured woollen stuff with a fitted bodice, a round flat-lying white collar and plain long sleeves, open and turned back at the wrists. A shoulder-shawl in a checked pattern of dull red and slate-blue is crossed over the chest. The underskirt of thick cotton stuff is striped in the same colours. The woman has pulled up the skirt of her dress to reach a canvas pocket attached to the waist of the underskirt and extract some money from it.

Stockings: These are of dove-grey wool.

Footwear: The woman wears practical bootees of fabric or leather with flat heels.

Accessories: A pair of scissors is attached to the outside of the pocket under the dress.

200. Guard of Stage-Coach. 1850

Hair: This is hardly seen under the hat, but is cut fairly short. Heavy side-whiskers are worn.

Headdress: The low-crowned top-hat has a curved brim.

Garments: The single-breasted overcoat is fastened with frogs and ends at the knees. The grey-brown trousers have straps under the feet. Both are probably of some water-proof material in a drab colour.

Footwear: The black leather boots are partially seen.

Accessories: The guard wears a leather strap from the right shoulder to the left hip, with a pouch for valuables or money. He carries a package belonging to a passenger in each hand.

CHAPTER NINE
1850–1890

The year 1848 was one of unrest in Europe, and revolutions occurred in France, Bohemia, Austria, Hungary and in some of the German States. In comparison, the situation in Great Britain was more stable. The long-term effect of the Industrial Revolution was to swing the balance of her economy towards industrialism. England needed vast quantities of raw materials from abroad to feed her manufacturing industries. Between 1850 and 1890, her lead in engineering and manufacturing industries and her ability to export her manufactured goods made her 'the workshop of the World'. The owners of mines and factories became very wealthy. Employment for ordinary workers was not difficult to find, but hours of daily work were long and pay was small. The poor remained poor.

A revolution in transport affected Britain as well as other countries. The railway systems were expanded, ensuring greater ease of travel. They carried some of the heavy loads previously confined to canals and rivers.

Following the work of Telford and McAdam, roads were gradually improved. The motor car had not yet arrived, but bicycles appeared. The Penny Farthing, a bicycle with wheels of unequal size, was soon replaced by a bicycle with wheels of equal size. Horse-drawn vehicles such as hansom cabs, hackney coaches, carts and gigs were used extensively. The underground Metropolitan Railway was opened in London in 1863, and the first Electric Tube Railway in 1890. Coal gas, mixed with air, was used in a gas engine. It was then found that a mixture of air and vaporised petrol was equally effective and the portable fuel necessary for a motor-car engine was evolved.

Large ocean-going ships, first made of iron and later of steel, were powered by steam. Britain's lead in shipbuilding enabled her to capture a large part of the world's carrying trade. The discovery of the uses of cold storage led to the provision of refrigerators in steamships. Meat, dairy produce and fruits could now be kept fresh during long sea voyages.

There was also a revolution in communications. The Penny Post had been introduced in 1840 and the Electric Telegraph Company had been formed in 1846. Samuel Morse invented the dot and dash alphabet called the Morse Code and a tapper to transmit it along a wire. Morse Code messages were sent by telegraph. In 1858 the first transatlantic cable was laid on the bed of the Atlantic Ocean, allowing telegraph messages to be sent between Britain and America. Later the invention of the telephone was followed by that of the phonograph. A typewriter in use in 1878 had a keyboard very like that of a typewriter of today.

The American, Edison, invented a glass vacuum bulb enclosing a carbon filament and made possible the development of electric light. Electric light was installed in 1880 on the Thames Embankment, in Victoria Station and in the British Museum. Gas lighting, however, continued to be used in Britain and other European countries for many years, in homes and in public.

Sir Robert Peel's police force, formed in 1829 in London, was the prototype of other police forces established in British towns which give the public a feeling of greater security.

Employment underground of women of any age and children under the age of ten had been forbidden in 1842, and by 1852 the employment of adult males underground came under the provision of the Mines Inspectorate. The use of little boys as chimney sweeps, thrust up through the chimneys armed with a sweeping brush, was made illegal by Acts of 1840 and 1864, but the prohibition was ignored in many places until a new Act in 1875 enforced it.

The Reform Bill of 1867 gave the franchise to working-class householders and the Education Act of 1870 provided for elementary education for all children between the ages of five and twelve. Children paid twopence each per week. Education was made compulsory in 1876 and free in 1891.

The Indian Mutiny brought the existence of the East India Company to an end, but British rule continued. The India Act brought India directly under the Crown. In later years India offered careers and commercial opportunities to civilians from Britain. From 1870 competitive examinations gave entry to the Civil Service, ensuring the choice of gifted young men for the bureaucracy.

Britain helped the Turks against the Russians in the Crimean War (1854–6). An English-woman, Florence Nightingale, organised hospitals in the Crimea for wounded soldiers. Her magnificent work and that of the nurses who helped her was the beginning of modern nursing. It proved the great value to society of the trained and educated woman, and was a step forward in her emancipation. In the last thirty years of the nineteenth century, education for girls was improved and women's colleges were founded. In 1871 the Married Women's Property Act enabled a woman to retain her own money instead of its passing to her husband.

Important discoveries were made in science and medicine. Louis Pasteur, a French chemist, discovered the tiny creatures called germs which cause disease and found a cure for anthrax. Joseph Lister, an English surgeon, used carbolic acid as a guard against germs infecting wounds and insisted on scrupulous cleanliness in hospitals.

The wealthy often built elaborately fashioned houses with every kind of turret, crenellation and over-embellishment that could be thought of, showing the lack of elegance and restraint that characterised architecture in the latter part of the nineteenth century. In the new industrial towns of the north, thousands of ugly little back-to-back terrace houses were erected to house the workers. They rapidly became overcrowded and developed into slums. In the later nineteenth century the rooms of middle-class houses were close-packed with masses of furniture, potted palms and aspidistras, overstuffed sofas and chairs. The closely draped windows often had coloured glass panes which shut out the light. Large over-decorated china and glass ornaments stood on fretwork brackets and big dark pictures made up further decoration.

In the 1870s the patenting of a successful carpet sweeper provided an early labour-saving device, the forerunner of many others. From the by-products of tar, itself a product of coal-gas manufacture, aniline dyes were fully developed.

Pioneers blazed trails westward in America and, braving attacks from Indians, built homes for themselves in this new territory. The Union Pacific Railway was constructed, joining the Atlantic and Pacific coasts of North America.

COSTUME OF THE PERIOD: 1850–1890

Hair—Men: Hair remained thick and rather long in the '50s, '60s and '70s, full at the sides with a side or centre parting. By the '80s it was usually cut short at the back. Whiskers were longer and thicker in the '50s, and in the '60s and '70s large and drooping. In the '80s large whiskers were mainly worn by elderly men, as were fringe beards joining moderate-sized whiskers.

After 1850 moustaches were bigger, the 'walrus' being a feature of the last two decades. Large beards were favoured from the '60s. They could be trimmed or left straggling. A 'spade' shape was frequently seen.

Hair—Women: In practical dress the general shape of elaborate coiffures was much simplified. In the '50s the parting was usually in the centre, with a wide formation of hair on each side. Braids or coils often crossed the top of the head, surrounding a flattened chignon of low or medium height. Side-ringlets, when worn, were arranged to contribute to the rounded shape.

In the early 1860s hair could be raised, unparted, from the forehead over a roll or pad showing the ears, and taken back to a chignon half-way up the head or to follow a drooping line. A set-back coronet of hair at the top of the head was often worn in the '70s. In the early '80s the coiffure was narrower with the chignon low down or at the crown of the head, and usually a fringe over the forehead. From about 1885 the chignon could be on the top of the head.

Headdress—Men: The top-hat was worn, with changes in height and shape, by men of varied occupations. The round felt hat with a pliable brim became the 'wide-awake' hat of the 1860s. The bowler hat, appearing at this time, had a tall crown at first, a low one in the '60s and first part of the '70s, a high one in the latter '70s and the '80s, and a moderate-sized one by 1890.

The stiff-brimmed straw hat and the small cloth cap were worn by all classes, including many tradesmen dealing in food, from the '70s onwards.

Headdress—Women: In the 1850s some bonnets hid the profile as in the '40s, but from 1850 into the '60s a face-framing shape set back on the head, with a smaller brim than formerly, was in fashion.

Hats with curved brims, usually dipping at the front and back, were also worn. A 'pork-pie' shape and another resembling a 'Glengarry' were examples of brimless hats. From the late '60s most headdress was perched on the now higher coiffure, upright or tilted forward, though some was set back.

Feathers, ribbon and artificial flowers trimmed the headdress, but it was much simplified for practical wear. Caps covered the head in the '50s, with ornament chiefly at the sides. In the '60s caps were set back, and in the '70s and '80s perched up.

Garments—Men: In the 1850s the frock-coat and the sloping-away coat were the main items of masculine fashion. Drab and neutral colouring was increasingly used.

The frock-coat was worn with striped, checked or otherwise patterned trousers by professional and business men, and upper tradesmen. During the decade the waistline became looser and the coat could end above the knees. The square-cut coat was now worn only as evening dress. It became the customary attire of waiters and butlers.

In the '60s short close-fitting jackets with matching trousers were the first recognisable examples of the lounge suit. From the '70s a sloping-away coat with short tails was worn in different materials, with non-matching trousers, by all classes of society.

Trousers fitted the leg fairly neatly in the '50s, covering the back of the shoes and part of the insteps. They were no longer strapped underfoot and were fuller in the leg after 1860. Knickerbocker suits were worn with gaiters by country people from the '70s.

Loosely fitting greatcoats ending at the knees were worn from the '50s, and long loose jackets by countrymen and gamekeepers. Waistcoats were usually lighter in colour than the coats, and could be striped, checked or variously patterned. They could match the coat and trousers from the 1860s.

Cravats with narrow ends tied in front were still seen in the '50s, but wide ties were now worn, often with a made-up bow.

The collar with points standing up against the jaws was worn by some men until the '60s. A high collar worn with a narrow tie and made-up bow or with an Ascot tie and tie-pin, a turned-over collar and a tie passed through a ring were innovations of the '50s. A low turned-over collar was a feature of the '60s and '70s. The wing-collar appeared in the '70s.

Garments—Women: The crinoline (a petticoat held out with cane or whalebone), which distended the bell-shaped skirt in the early 1850s, was not often used for active work, the dress being worn over petticoats.

Long close sleeves could be worn throughout the period with working dress, but three-quarter length ones, loose and frilled or with 'bishop' sleeves to the wrist emerging at their ends, were now in fashion.

The circumference of the skirt was larger in the late '50s and early '60s. A plain, front-buttoned close-fitting bodice could be worn during the period for practical work. By 1866 the size of the skirt was diminishing. In 1870 the bustle appeared at the back of a slightly high waistline. For active pursuits it was not large, and the underskirt, showing beneath the open drawn-back overskirt, could clear the ground.

In 1875 a long bodice fitted the figure, covering the hips. The bustle became smaller and lower, the overskirt was draped back apron-fashion, and both skirts were narrower. The tied-back skirt took various forms in the next thirteen years or so. In 1883 there was a return to the large bustle, now jutting out from the back of a rather low waist, but this was minimised in utilitarian dress. By 1886 some skirts were not draped in front, and 1889 a change in the fashions had begun.

Shoes—Men: Shoes laced in front had appeared by 1860, and patent leather a little earlier.

Boots—Men: Leather bootees, sometimes with cloth uppers, and elastic gussets from 1847, continued to be the main item of men's footwear. Black or brown leather boots lacing in front were worn in the country from the '70s onwards, with thick woollen stockings and often with gaiters added. Labourers wore large thick-soled versions of these.

Shoes—Women: Women still wore thin-soled slippers in the '50s, with slightly raised heels.

Boots—Women: Bootees were laced on the inside when not gusseted with elastic. Small shaped heels were worn by the '70s. Boots were laced in front or buttoned at the sides during the '70s and '80s.

Materials, Colours and Ornament: Materials used included all kinds of cloth, velveteen, corduroy and homespun, with durable cottons, poplins, linen and some silk and muslin. Colours were sober in the main, but the aniline dyes discovered in the '50s provided some vivid hues. Trimming for women's dress included fringe, buttons, contrasting stuffs, piping and ruching. Men had tiepins, studs, watches and chains. Women wore brooches to fasten the collar, and those in business or the few professions open to them watches and inconspicuous jewellery.

201. Town Labourer with Pick-Axe. 1850–60

Hair: The hair is thick and slightly long.

Headdress: The cap resembles a 'deer-stalker' in green tweed, with a tassel on the top.

Garments: The man wears a tunic-shaped shirt of blue-and-white checked cotton, with the sleeves rolled up. It is belted and open-necked, showing part of the front of the vest. The breeches are close-fitting, made of brown worsted, and end at the calves, where they are laced at the front. A stout belt can be seen where the shirt is open down the front.

Stockings: Thick brownish-grey woollen stockings are worn.

Boots: These are of tough leather, very stout and heavy, with thick soles. They are laced up the front.

Accessories: The labourer is holding a pick-axe.

202. Maid-Servant. 1850–60

Hair: The hair is put up in a small chignon fairly high at the back of the head. A ringlet hangs on each side in front of the ear.

Headdress: The white muslin cap is set back on the head and has a long ear-piece on each side hanging over the cheeks and temples.

Garments: The printed cotton dress has a fitted bodice and a bell-shaped skirt worn over petticoats. It has long plain loosely fitting sleeves. The large white muslin apron has no bib.

Shoes: The flat-soled slippers are of black leather.

203. Town Labourer. 1850s–'60s

Hair. The hair is cut short but is fairly thick. Side-whiskers are worn.

Headdress: A small blue cloth cap is put on with the peak a little to one side.

Garments: The man wears a white shirt with the sleeves rolled up. The turned-down collar buttons at the neck. His dun-coloured trousers are kept up by a leather belt. He wears a rather long white apron. Both this and the shirt are discoloured by wear and the nature of the work he does.

Footwear: He wears thick-soled boots.

Accessories: The man is wielding a heavy industrial hammer.

204. Man in Soup-Kitchen. About 1860

Hair: The hair is roughly cut and is hardly seen.

Headdress: The brown cloth cap resembles a forage-cap.

Garments: The man wears a red muffler and a red-and-blue striped cotton shirt with sleeves rolled up, and rather shapeless dark-grey trousers of the period, in this case of cheap rough-surfaced cloth. Over these he wears a coarse sacking apron.

Footwear: His heavy boots are of black leather.

Accessories: The man carries two buckets of hot soup ready for serving.

205. Woman Serving in a Soup-Kitchen. About 1860

Hair: The hair is parted in the centre and is done in a fairly low chignon (unseen).

Headdress: A red-and-white patterned scarf, folded cornerwise, has been tied over the head.

Garments: The faded red cotton bodice has no visible collar, and the long sleeves fit closely at the wrist. A small fringed yellow and red shawl, folded into a triangle, is worn crossed over the chest. The dark-blue bell-shaped skirt is put on over petticoats. A white apron with two bands at the back to keep it in place is worn.

Footwear: The black list slippers have flat soles.

Accessories: The woman is serving soup to a crowd of poor people, and is using a long-handled saucepan to pour it into a bowl.

206. Gold-Mining Prospector. 1860s

Hair: This is cut short and almost hidden by the cap.

Headdress: The blue cloth rimless cap has a peak in front.

Garments: The prospector wears a short jacket of blue frieze, with the sleeves made in one with it. The trousers are of rough grey cloth. A revolver in its holster is attached to a strong leather belt.

Boots: These are of black leather.

Accessories: The man carries a curiously shaped spade with a long haft.

207. Peasant Woman Baking Bread. 1860s–'70s

Hair: This is hidden under the cap.

Headdress: The woollen cap is of soft parchment-coloured wool. The fullness in the crown has been pushed backward over her head.

Garments: The sleeves of the white cotton blouse are rolled up. Over it is worn a greenish-blue sleeveless woollen jacket ending at the waist. The over-skirt is of light-brown wool, and has been turned up and pinned at the back, showing the under-skirt of maroon-coloured wool or thick cotton. The costume could be worn by women of many countrified, seafaring or remote districts.

Footwear: Thick-soled natural leather mules are worn over bare feet.

Accessories: The woman is holding a long-handled iron shovel with a loaf on it ready for baking in a brick oven.

208. Cook in Printed Dress. 1864

Hair: The hair is parted in the centre and looped to give a wide effect before being formed into a flattened chignon at the back.

Headdress: The cap is of white cambric.

Garments: The dress is of printed cotton in blue and white. It has a fitted bodice with a round flat white collar. The skirt is worn over a moderate-sized crinoline. The full-length sleeves are full and are sewn into a band at the wrists, where narrow white cuffs are added. The white cooking-apron is held up by clasps on the shoulders and protects most of the dress.

Footwear: Flat black slippers are worn but hardly seen.

Accessories: The cook is holding a bowl and a wooden spoon.

209. Man in Short Frock-Coat. About 1870

Hair: The hair is fairly thick and the back of it is seen under the hat. A moustache and whiskers are worn.

Headdress: The black top-hat is worn at an angle and tilted forward.

Garments: The black frock-coat has short skirts and high lapels. It is worn fastened. The black striped trousers widen slightly at the bottom. A stiff winged collar and black bow-tie are worn.

Boots: These are black leather bootees with elastic gussets (unseen).

Accessories: The man carries a malacca walking-stick with a silver knob at the top.

210. Photographer. 1870s

Hair: The hair is cut short but is very thick and curly all over the head.

Garments: The grey lounge suit is worn with a matching waistcoat. The coat is curved at the hem in front. The suit has an ill-fitting look and is pulled and wrinkled by the man's movements. He wears a low turned-down collar and a floppy bow tie.

Footwear: Black leather bootees are worn. Their tops are hidden by the trousers.

Accessories: The photographer is holding the apparatus by which sitters' heads were kept in the required position.

211. Street-Corner Loafer. 1870s

Hair: The hair is cut short and the man is clean-shaven.

Headdress: A bowler hat with a tall crown is worn.

Garments: The man wears a black short-tailed coat with skirts put on at the waist. It was worn by all classes from the 1870s until the first decade of the 1900s. The black-and-grey checked trousers are baggy in a passing fashion of the 1870s. A woollen muffler is worn in place of a collar.

Shoes: Shabby black leather boots are worn.

Accessories: The man carries a cane.

212. Irish Peat-Cutter. 1870s

Hair: The hair is drawn back into a low chignon with a fringe over the brow.

Garments: The blouse of shabby green cotton stuff has three-quarter length sleeves without cuffs or other finish. A red-and-pink fringed woollen shawl is crossed over on the bosom. The striped skirt of dull green and blue serge is worn over petticoats.

Footwear: The legs and feet are bare.

Accessories: The girl carries on her back a specially shaped basket containing slabs of peat which she has cut.

213. Coachman. About 1870

Hair: The hair is cut short, with a side-parting (unseen).

Headdress: The top-hat of shiny black plush has a wheel-shaped black silk cockade on the left side.

Garments: The coachman wears a double-breasted caped overcoat, slightly shaped to the figure, of dark-green cloth piped in buff-yellow. His matching trousers partly cover his boots.

Boots: The boots of black leather end (unseen) at the ankles.

Accessories: The coachman is holding a whip.

214. Parlour-Maid. 1870–80

Hair: The hair is parted in the centre and drawn back into a chignon at the back of the head.

Headdress: A white lawn cap is perched on the top of the head.

Garments: The black dress has a fitted bodice fastened down the front (unseen). The collar has a white frill and the close-fitting sleeves are plain. The skirt shows the shoes, and is made with a slight fullness at the back below the waist. A white apron without a bib is worn.

Shoes: Black slippers with low heels are worn.

Accessories: The maid is arranging small cakes on a pedestal dish.

215. Schoolgirl. 1875

Hair: The hair is drawn back unparted and tied with a black ribbon bow at the crown of the head. The remainder is allowed to hang down the back and is tied by a second bow at the shoulder-blades.

Garments: The girl wears a dress of wine-red cashmere with a white collar fastened by a brooch at the base of the throat. It has a matching sash draped at the back in imitation of the grown-up mode. The skirt ends at the calves. The white apron has a plain square neckline with frills at the shoulders and all round the skirt. It is tied at the back of the waist and the shoulder-pieces continue crossed-over at the back and buttoned to the waist-belt of the apron.

Stockings: The stockings are black cashmere or thin cotton.

Shoes: The 'court'-shaped black kid slippers have small shaped heels.

Accessories: The girl is reading a book that she carries.

216. Policeman. 1878

Hair: The hair is cut short.

Headdress: The dark-blue conical helmet has a silver badge in front.

Garments: The long overcoat of dark-blue cloth ends at mid-calf. It has a high collar, buttons down the front to the waist, a dark-blue and white armlet above the right wrist and a black leather belt to which the truncheon is attached. The trousers match the overcoat.

Footwear: The boots are of black leather.

Accessories: The policeman carries a lantern, which is hooked to the left front of the belt when not in use.

217. Footman. 1880

Hair: The straight hair is parted in the centre and combed downwards.

Garments: The footman wears a dark-blue tail-coat, cut square at the waist, and matching trousers. The collar and cuffs are red and there is a red stripe down the outside of the trousers. The dark-blue and white striped waistcoat is unseen. A white starched collar and white bow-tie are worn.

Footwear: The bootees, with tops covered by the trousers, are of black leather.

Accessories: The footman is holding a silver salver.

218. Gardener. 1880s

Hair: This is cut short and hardly shows under the hat. Side-whiskers are worn.

Headdress: The gardener wears a straw 'boater' with a black band.

Garments: The blue-and-white striped flannel shirt is worn without a collar and is fastened with a stud. The sleeves are rolled up. Grey flannel trousers and a grey waistcoat are worn. The green baize apron has two large pockets in front.

Footwear: The boots are of black leather.

Accessories: The apron-pockets hold twine and other gardening necessities. The gardener is holding a pot-plant.

219. American Farm-Boy. 1880s

Hair: This is thick, straight, and long enough to cover the ears.

Headdress: The straw hat has a shallow crown and large brim.

Garments: The boy wears an open-necked white cotton shirt and braces supporting his blue denim trousers.

Footwear: The shoes are of grey canvas and rubber.

Accessories: The boy is carrying a hoe.

220. American Country Schoolgirl. 1885

Hair: This is parted in the centre behind a thick fringe over the forehead, and plaited to hang down the back.

Garments: The girl wears a dress of soft green serge, with a narrow white collar fastened with a brooch (unseen) at the base of the throat. It has plain wrist-length sleeves and a little fullness at the back of the waist (unseen). The skirt ends at the ankles. The white calico pinafore covers most of the dress. It is frilled at the arm-openings and round the wide neckline. It is fastened by two or three buttons at the back of the shoulders and again at the waist by ties of its own material attached at the side-seams.

Footwear: The bootees are of black leather. Black stockings (unseen) are worn.

221. Girl Clerk working at U.S. Treasury. 1885

Hair: The hair is cut in a fringe in front and dressed in a chignon on the top of the head (unseen).

Headdress: The hat has a tall, diminishing crown and is worn straight on the head, while the brim is curved. It is of black velvet and has an ornament of wide leaf-brown taffetas ribbon in front.

Garments: The figure-fitting high-collared jacket is of black velvet, ending at the hips and fastening down the front. The dress, of leaf-brown silk, is draped into a moderate bustle shape at the back. Only its skirt is shown.

Shoes: Black kid shoes can be partly seen.

Accessories: The girl carries a black silk umbrella ornamented with a black ribbon bow, and wears biscuit-coloured kid gloves.

222. American Housekeeper with Lamp. 1885

Hair: The hair is parted in the centre and drawn into a low chignon at the back.

Headdress: The white lawn cap has a frilled edge and a crown higher in front than at the back.

Garments: The serviceable dress is of dark-blue cashmere. It has a fitted bodice to the hips, buttoning down the front, with a small upstanding collar fastened in front by a brooch. The plain three-quarter length sleeves are finished with white frilling and a band of silk braid matching the dress. The hips are swathed in folds of the dark-blue stuff which is draped into a small bustle effect (unseen) at the back. The skirt just clears the ground and is trimmed with two rows of the silk braid.

Footwear: Part of the black leather slippers is seen.

Accessories: The woman carries a paraffin lamp with a frosted glass globe and a brass stand.

223. Elderly American Fisherman or Wharfman. 1885

Hair: The grey hair is fairly thick.

Headdress: The hat is of light-brown felt, with a high soft crown and the brim turned down all round.

Garments: The loosely fitting jacket is of brown hopsack or worsted, with a patch on one elbow and pockets near the front. The waistcoat is of a lighter brown. The trousers are almost hidden by overalls of waterproofed stuff, patched at the knee and worn rather short.

Footwear: Stout leather boots are worn.

Accessories: The man carries a walking-stick.

224. American Farmer. 1880s

Hair: The hair is thick and fairly short. A moustache and beard are worn.

Headdress: The low-crowned hat of parchment-coloured felt has a wide brim rolled upward at the sides.

Garments: The farmer is dressed for attending an agricultural auction. The black frock-coat can be worn for riding and ends below the knees. The trousers are striped in black and grey.

Footwear: The bootees of black leather have heels suitable for riding.

Accessories: The farmer is carrying a riding-crop.

225. General Domestic Help. 1885

Hair: The hair is dressed in a bun low down at the back of the head (unseen) and is cut in a fringe in front with a centre-parting.

Garments: The dark-maroon alpaca dress has the sleeves rolled up. It has a fitted bodice fastened down the front with a small high collar. A large white apron hides most of the skirt, which clears the ground and is bordered with a frill of its own stuff.

Footwear: The black shoes or bootees are hardly seen.

Accessories: The woman is pouring coffee into a cup from a large metal coffee-pot. This dress would be suitable for a general domestic help, for a working-class housewife or other practically occupied woman.

CHAPTER TEN
1890–1910

'La Belle Époque' is a fitting name for the last decade of the nineteenth century and the first of the twentieth, suggesting the sophistication and love of luxury that were its outstanding characteristics.

It was a time of lavish expenditure in the realm of social enjoyment. The fashionable house-parties, gatherings for race-meetings and the visits to Continental cities and spas were whole-time occupations for the rich. This way of living made profit for tradesmen and work for a vast number of servants.

The staff of a large country house would include more footmen and housemaids than were needed in a town establishment. In addition to the butler, housekeeper, cook, valet, lady's maid, laundress, kitchen-maid and scullery-maid normally employed, there would be a man or boy to clean the knives, bring in coals and wait on the servants' hall and house-keeper's room. There would also be a coachman, or chauffeur after the coming of the motor car, and grooms and gardeners. A maid would wait on the schoolroom and another on the nursery.

Whether in town or in the country, many children of wealthy families saw little of their parents until they were well into their teens, except when they 'came down to dessert' at the end of dinner or during 'children's hour' after tea, when they went down to the drawing-room to spend a little time with them. From the nursery, they graduated to the schoolroom, living their daily life with the governess instead of the nurse. This meant a régime of lessons, walks in the grounds or sedate games in London parks and gardens, and friendships with other children in the same milieu. When a house-party was being entertained, there were often the valets, ladies' maids, and children's nurses of visitors to swell the numbers in the servants' hall.

Everyone dressed for dinner, formally in great houses, and in simpler dresses in smaller houses or rectories. Going down to dinner meant a chilly journey, for passages and staircases were unheated.

Large country houses often generated their own electricity, if their owners could afford to do so. Gas was laid on where it could be obtained, and elsewhere paraffin lamps were used. Bedroom candlesticks were set out in the hall of a country house for family and guests to take up to their rooms at night. Cans of hot water were taken up for the hip-baths which were put in the bedrooms in houses which as yet had no bathrooms, and the washstands in the bedrooms were supplied with hot water several times a day. In the large terrace-houses, of which there are still so many in central London, families would entertain a great deal. The drawing-room had double doors between the two sections that could be folded back to make one large room for use as a ballroom, or for concerts and parties.

In the cities, the humbler classes had the public-houses, the music-halls, the naphtha-flared markets and the enticing shops to enjoy in their leisure time. A rare visit to the pit or gallery of a theatre would bring them a light opera or, in the 1900s, one of the musical comedies whose stars and music are still remembered. A splendid Shakespearean production, or one of the new plays of Ibsen or Shaw, would be another possible choice.

Scientific discovery and invention advanced at a tremendous pace. In 1893, a carburetter resembling that of today was used in motor-cars; the first films were shown in 1895, and X-rays discovered in the same year.

In 1900, a form of tape recorder known as a 'telegraphone' was demonstrated at the Paris Exhibition. In 1905, Einstein stated his first theory of relativity. The Wright brothers flew their aeroplane in 1903, and in 1904, Rutherford and Soddy stated the general theory of radio-activity, opening the way to the exploration of the atom and its energy.

COSTUME OF THE PERIOD: 1890–1910

Hair—Men: Men's hair was cut short at the back and could be parted at the side, often with an upstanding quiff, or in the centre, pressed down on the forehead on each side and either brushed back over the ears or pressed down all round. Moustaches, sideburns, large side-whiskers and beards of all types were worn.

Hair—Women: A small coiffure drawn up to the top of the head, usually with a fringe in front and leaving the ears exposed, was fashionable until the mid-'90s. A softer line was also developed, with a pompadour and a high or low chignon. By 1908 puffs at the sides were more usual than a pompadour. Combs, pins and pads were used to keep the coiffure in place, and curl-papers were necessary until the invention of Marcel-waving in 1907.

Headdress—Men: The top-hat continued to be worn for most social occasions and by business and professional men, by undertakers and some cabmen, shop-assistants and clerical workers. Farmers and other country people wore a low-crowned version of this. The bowler hat had a crown of moderate height and was worn by tradesmen, business-men, servants, clerical workers, artisans and some labourers.

The straw 'boater' was worn by men of all occupations. Butchers, fishmongers, gardeners and some street-traders wore it as a sign of their calling.

Small close-fitting cloth or tweed caps continued to be worn by all classes, the gentry adopting it for country pursuits. Tweed hats with narrow turned-down brims were worn by working-men as well as by gentry in the country. The 'Homburg' hat was worn mainly by the leisured classes. (See 'Headdress—Women'.)

Headdress—Women: Most women's hats were perched on the head and decorated with feathers, ribbons and flowers. They had moderate brims in the 1890s, often turned up at the back. Toques and bonnets, the latter set back on the head, were worn in both decades, the latter unfashionably in the 1900s. Larger brims and a greater variety of styles were characteristic from the later '90s. By 1908 picture-hats and larger toques were in favour.

A feminine version of the staw 'boater' was worn with plain dress and an imitation of the masculine 'Homburg' for women, including some school-mistresses and those employed in business who admired the mannish mode.

Garments—Men: The frock-coat was still worn by lawyers, doctors and other professional and business men. The 'sloping-away' coat with matching or different-coloured trousers was still an outfit for all classes. The morning-coat that developed from it was fastened with three buttons. The lounge suit was worn by men in a large variety of occupations. The short lapels were superseded by longer ones from 1904.

Loosely fitting tweed jackets and non-matching trousers or knickerbockers were worn by country people. Trousers were of the same medium width all the way down in the 1890s. The crease down the front was worn from about 1895. They fitted rather more neatly in the early 1900s, just covering the tops of the shoes, until the turn-up was first worn in 1903. Improved manufacture of raincoats and lighter overcoats made the heavy coats of the former decade less necessary.

Garments—Women: A long-waisted, tightly corseted upright figure was fashionable in 1890, with skirts of moderate width carrying some fullness at the back. By 1895 a trim, boned bodice with a normal waist-level, side shoulders and flared circular skirts provided a prettier fashion.

The coat-and-skirt was develped as a basic outfit at this time. At the turn of the century a change in the line of corsetry encouraged women to lean forward from the widened hips.

A long forward-thrust bustline with, until 1906, a deeply pouched bodice and downward-pointing waistbelt added to the artificiality of the posture. Practical dress was not unduly influenced by the ultra-fashionable line, since women found it possible to remain comfortably upright in the long curved corset, which gave admirable support.

High collars were worn almost invariably with day-dresses. Stiff masculine double collars with bow-ties were an item of smart dress, and were worn by waitresses and parlour-maids. Sleeves were long and close-fitting in 1890, with raised and gathered shoulders. During the next five years many became more elaborate, with large shoulder-puffs and lower sleeves tapering to the wrists. An alternative in 1906–7 was a drooping 'bishop-type' sleeve set in below the shoulder. Three-quarter or elbow-length sleeves, often ending in frills, were in fashion from 1904 onwards.

In 1908 dresses with straight or moderately flared skirts and some with higher waists appeared. The shoulder-line was normal and some long sleeves were worn, though elbow- and three-quarter length ones were still in vogue. The long stays now showed less exaggerated lines.

Hose and Footwear—Men: Men's socks were of neutral colours, and were made of wool, cashmere, cotton and silk. Thick woollen stockings, often with gaiters over them, were worn with knickerbockers and boots.

Laced leather boots, ending above the ankle, were worn generally by men engaged in all types of work. Shoes became more popular during the early 1900s.

Hose and Footwear––Women: Women's stockings were black, or occasionally brown, and made of wool, cotton or silk. Laced or buttoned leather boots, ending at the calf, were worn by most women. Leather slippers made in 'Court' shape or with straps across the insteps and moderate or low heels were worn in the house, and laced shoes out of doors from about 1900.

Materials, Colours and Ornament: Cloth, serge, tweed, check suiting, worsted, homespun (and corduroy for the trousers and waistcoats, with flannel for the shirts of labourers) were among the materials used in the maufacture of men's clothes. Serge or inexpensive cloth was worn by women for dresses and coats-and-skirts, with thin woollen fabrics or printed or plain cotton for blouses and summer dresses.

Colours in the '90s were more subtle and sophisticated than in the preceding decade, and many nuances were introduced. These found their way to the clothes of functionaries, especially those who bought clothes second-hand or had them provided by employers or other donors.

Ornament among manual workers was restricted to simple embellishments like decorative buttons, artificial flowers, ribbons and bead necklaces for women, and steel-studded belts and bright neckerchiefs for men.

Jewellery and Accessories: Jewellery was not much worn with working dress, but in commerce and the professions a small show of such objects as gold signet rings and watch-chains, lockets and brooches could be made.

Women did not often carry handbags, but kept a purse in a pocket, in the seam of a skirt or attached to a webbing belt under it. The handbag was more generally in use by 1910.

Umbrellas were carried by men and women, and most men had a walking-stick or, in the country, a stout ash-plant. Gloves were of wool, cotton, silk or leather.

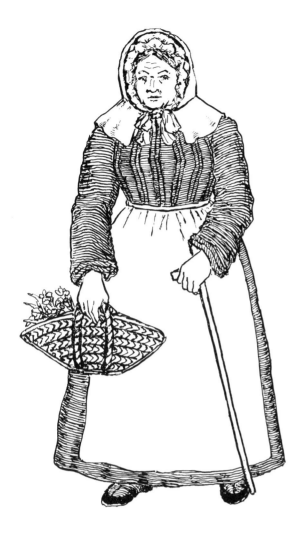

226. Elderly Countrywoman. About 1890

Hair: The hair is parted in the centre, with ringlets at the temples.

Headdress: The old woman wears a pink cotton sunbonnet over a white cap with a frill in front.

Garments: Her worn dress of faded pink-and-red cotton has a fitted bodice and a plain, fairly full skirt worn over petticoats. Her long sleeves are shapeless with wear and have no cuffs. She wears a white apron.

Shoes: Shabby, practically shaped shoes of black leather are worn.

Accessories: The woman holds a walking-stick and a basket of flowers.

227. Woman and Boy Slum-Dwellers. 1890

Hair: The woman's hair is straight and unkempt, hanging down raggedly under her hat. The boy has thick, rather long hair overhanging his eyes in a fringe.

Headdress: The hat is of black straw in the shape of a 'boater' with a black ribbon round it tied in a double bow with the ends upstanding.

Garments: The woman is wearing a shabby blouse of faded pink silk with puffed sleeves ending at the elbow. An old narrow scarf of blue wool is tied round her neck under the collar. The ancient black skirt dips at the back. She wears a white apron. The boy wears a white cotton shirt with sleeves rolled up, an open waistcoat and trousers braced very high and rolled up at the bottom. All these garments are too large for him.

Footwear: The woman has on broken black boots. The boy is barefoot.

Accessories: The woman is holding a mug of beer. She probably earns a little by cleaning-jobs and the boy runs errands for pennies.

228. Scottish Boy Working as a Golf-Caddie. 1890

Hair: The boy's hair is cut short.

Headdress: The Scots 'bonnet' is of dark blue, with black ribbons hanging at the back and a red pompon on the top.

Garments: The boy wears a brown jacket and has a piece of red ribbon tied round his neck in a bow. His matching trousers are rolled up.

Footwear: The feet are bare.

Accessories: The boy is carrying three golf-clubs.

229. Street or Public-House Character. 1890

Hair: This shows very little and is cut short at back and sides. Whiskers are worn.

Headdress: A bowler hat with a crown of moderate height is worn.

Garments: The overcoat is of fairly thick cloth of an in-determinate dark-drab colour. A faded green woollen muffler is folded round the neck. The trousers are of a dim buff-yellow-and-brown check.

Boots: The serviceable boots are of black leather.

Accessories: The man is carrying a stout stick.

230. Old Countryman. 1890s

Hair: The hair is comparatively thick, cut short and hidden by the hat. Side-whiskers are worn.

Headdress: The ancient hat is of green tweed, with a soft crown and the brim turned downward.

Garments: The loose thigh-length coat is of greenish-grey homespun and the trousers of mole-coloured corduroy, with patched knees. The striped waistcoat is an ancient 'fancy' one striped in green and grey. The muffler round his neck is buff-coloured with brown spots.

Footwear: Stout boots are worn.

Accessories: The man carries a trug containing vegetables.

231. Two Slatternly Women. 1890s

Hair: The hair of the taller woman is dressed in a ragged fringe in front and pulled into a knot at the back. The girl's hair is also untidily fringed.

Garments: The taller woman wears a worn-out pink silk blouse and a checked shawl in red, black and white. Her skirt is part of a puce taffeta crinoline dress, without the crinoline and with the hem unevenly taken up in tucks. The girl wears a shabby brown silk dress of the 1880s, the bodice gaping and the skirt trailing at the back.

Shoes: The taller woman is barefoot and the girl wears broken black boots.

232. Nursing Sister. 1890s

Hair: The hair is dressed in a curling fringe in front and a rather low chignon at the back.

Headdress: The starched white muslin cap fits the back of the head and has two rows of pleated frills, one above the forehead and another over the crown of the head.

Garments: The deep-blue uniform dress has long sleeves and a starched white collar and cuffs. A starched white belt is worn over the white apron.

Footwear: Low-heeled black shoes are worn over black stockings (unseen).

Accessories: The sister is holding a sheaf of papers in one hand and a watch on a chain attached to her belt in the other. The watch is ordinarily kept tucked into it.

233. Flashy Town Character. 1890s

Hair: This is arranged with a quiff pressed down on to the forehead. A full moustache is worn.

Headdress: The black top-hat has been pushed to the back of the head.

Garments: The short-jacketed lounge suit is of grey suiting and the waistcoat of pearl-grey faced cloth.

Footwear: The boots are of black leather.

Accessories: The man holds a cigar in his left hand.

234. American Hunter. 1890s

Hair: This is thick but not worn long.

Headdress: The wide-brimmed black felt hat is turned back from the face.

Garments: The loose green-dyed leather jacket has leather fringes on the outside of the sleeves at the point below the shoulders where these are put in, and round the lower edge. The trousers are of rough woollen stuff in a neutral faded blue-green.

Footwear: Stout light-brown leather boots are worn, ending below the knees.

Accessories: The hunter carries a shotgun.

235. Woman Journeying to the Yukon. 1898

Hair: The hair is taken back from the face above the ears and put up in an untidy bun at the back.

Headdress: The woman wears a small version of a man's Homburg hat, part of the mannish mode. It is battered as a result of the hardships of the journey.

Garments: The grey tailored jacket has puffed shoulders and is flared over the hips. The dark-green skirt has been cut short to make walking easier on hard, rough ground.

Footwear: The boots are large and strongly made, the same as those worn by men during part of the journey on foot to join the Gold Rush.

Accessories: The woman carries a roughly shaped wooden staff.

236. Woman with Bundle of Rags. About 1900

Hair: The straight uncared-for hair is parted in the centre and pulled into a small bun at the back. There is a ragged fringe over the forehead.

Garments: A shrunken blouse or old bodice in faded neutral colour is fastened in front. Its sleeves are rolled up. A length of sacking has been draped round the hips to cover rents in the ragged black skirt.

Footwear: The bare feet are thrust into old and broken black boots without laces.

Accessories: The woman, a slum-dweller, is carrying a heavy bundle of old rags tied up in a sheet or tablecloth.

237. Scotswoman Selling Salt Fish. About 1900

Hair: This is parted in the centre. Only a little of it can be seen.

Headdress: The frill of a white cap framing the face can be partly seen. A small patterned kerchief in red and grey, with a fringed edge, is tied over this.

Garments: The white blouse has a pattern of small black dots. It fits the figure and has plain sleeves, loose at the wrists and without cuffs. The light-yellow skirt of thick cotton stuff is turned up, showing the red-and-white striped lining. The underskirt is of grey woollen stuff, and the cloak of black serge.

Stockings: These are of coarse grey yarn.

Shoes: Low-heeled black leather shoes are worn.

Accessories: The woman has a walking-stick with a crooked handle, covered by her hand. She carries a large basket, woven over osier stems, covered by an old brown blanket or piece of canvas. Salted herring are in the basket, which is fastened to her back by a webbing band which goes round her forehead.

238. Muffin-Man. 1900

Hair: The hair is cut short and the man wears a moustache of the 'walrus' type.

Headdress: He is wearing a small grey cloth cap.

Garments: The shabby lounge suit is brownish-drab in colour and the waistcoat a faded grey. The man wears a narrow red muffler round his neck inside the collar.

Footwear: The stout boots are of black leather.

Accessories: The man is carrying a handbell with which to announce his wares and on his head a wooden tray of muffins, covered with a cloth. A black cotton pad covers the top of his head to balance the tray.

239. Girl Type-Setter on American Country Newspaper. 1900

Hair: The hair is arranged in a moderate pompadour and a fringe in front. It is plaited and doubled under at the back and tied with a black ribbon.

Garments: The dress is of light-blue cashmere, made with a yoke and three tucks close together set vertically down the front and back of the bodice. The sleeves are full at the top and have detachable black over-sleeves put on above the elbows. The skirt is flared a little, with some fullness at the back of the waist, and ends above the ankles. The white starched collar is finished by a black bow. A black apron is worn.

Stockings: The stockings (unseen) are of fine black wool.

Footwear: Bootees of black leather with moderate heels are worn.

240. Postman. 1900

Hair: The hair is cut short. A small moustache is worn.

Headdress: The postman has a cap with a peak in front and a downward curve at the back. There is a silver badge on the front.

Garments: The dark-blue coat has small lapels and is worn with a wing-collar and dark-coloured tie. The coat has brass buttons and silver badges on the collar. The trousers, matching the coat, cover part of the boots.

Footwear: Stout black leather boots are worn.

Accessories: The postman has a canvas bag containing letters slung from right shoulder to left hip. He is holding a letter in his hand.

241. Parlourmaid. 1900

Hair: The hair is worn in a moderate pompadour in front and is swept up at the back into a small chignon within the cap.

Headdress: The starched white muslin cap is arranged in upright pleated frills on the top of the head and has long streamers at the back.

Garments: The black dress has a neatly fitting bodice and flared skirt just clearing the ground. It is worn with a high starched collar, a made-up white bow tie and a white apron with a bib, tied at the back of the waist in a bow with long ends. The sleeves have white starched cuffs.

Footwear: Black shoes and stockings are worn.

Accessories: The parlourmaid carries a tray with two glasses on it.

242. Cowboy. Early 1900s

Hair: This is cut short and does not show much under the hat-brim.

Headdress: The typical cowboy hat with a flat circular brim and moderate-sized crown is worn.

Garments: The loose open jacket is of dun-coloured wool suiting. A yellow-and-black patterned silk scarf is tied round the neck, with one end thrown back over the right shoulder. The trousers are of light-brown leather, with leather fringes down the sides. Two flap-pockets are attached to the front of the trousers near the top. Each has leather fringes at its rounded base and the edge of the flap.

Footwear: High-heeled spurred riding-boots are worn under the trousers.

Accessories: A revolver-holster attached to a black leather belt can be seen under the edge of the coat and the man has just drawn his revolver.

243. Milliner. 1903

Hair: The hair is dressed in a pompadour in front and taken up at the back to a chignon on the top of the head.

Garments: The black dress of silk or soft thin woollen stuff has a deeply bloused bodice and a long flared skirt sweeping the ground. The chemisette within the neckline is boned to form a high collar. The belt is shaped into a downward point in front. The sleeves droop from the shoulders to some fullness on the forearms, where close-fitting sleeve-ends are attached.

Footwear: The toe of one black kid slipper can be seen.

Accessories: The milliner wears a brooch at the throat of her dress. She is showing a fashionable hat, trimmed with feathers and ribbon, to a customer.

244. Girl Wearing Straw 'Boater'. 1904

Hair: The hair is parted in the centre and puffed out at the sides. The chignon is fairly high at the back, jutting out to support the hat.

Headdress: The straw 'boater' has a dark-blue ribbon round it.

Garments: The white lawn blouse has a high turned-over collar and is worn with a wide dark-blue silk tie. The sleeves have fullness at the elbows with close-fitting lower sleeves attached. These are cut in a pointed shape at the join. A buckled belt of dark-blue leather is worn. The pleated skirt is of dark-blue serge and just shows the shoes. It is of the type worn for active pursuits. A blouse and skirt, hat and gloves were considered suitable for going out in summer weather. This might be worn by a governess, schoolmistress, secretary, university student or social worker.

Footwear: Laced black boots with small shaped heels are worn.

Accessories: The girl wears gloves and is carrying a small case, unusual at this time, which might contain notebooks and writing material.

245. Woman in Coat and Skirt. 1905

Hair: The hair is taken up at the back and dressed in a pompadour in front (unseen).

Headdress: The hat of dark-purple velvet over a buckram foundation is oval in shape without a brim, and is perched up on the head and tipped forward. A bunch of small grey feathers is set upright at the back.

Garments: The figure-fitting jacket of dark-purple faced cloth ends at the hips. Its sleeves widen towards the wrists. A blouse is worn beneath it but is not seen. The skirt is widely flared and very long. A neckpiece or tippet of grey feathers is worn round the neck and tied in front with purple ribbon.

Shoes: Part of one laced black walking-shoe can be seen.

Accessories: The woman is wearing pearl-grey kid gloves and carries an umbrella in her left hand. The right hand is used for holding up her long flared skirt.

246. Housemaid. 1907

Hair: The straight, rather untidy hair is pulled tightly into a knot fairly high at the back of the head.

Headdress: A cap made of a starched frill of white cotton, pulled into a small shape with a draw-string, is perched on the top of the head.

Garments: The full-skirted dress of blue-and-white printed cotton ends just above the shoes. It has rolled-up sleeves and a starched high white collar. A large white bibbed apron is also worn.

Footwear: Black fabric bootees with leather toe-caps and black stockings (unseen) are worn.

Accessories: The housemaid is sweeping the floor with a broom.

247. Elderly Country Carrier. 1907

Hair: The hair is raggedly cut and the side-whiskers untrimmed.

Headdress: The peaked cap is of soft dark-blue material with the back turned up and buttoned to the crown.

Garments: The loose jacket is of brown worsted. The grey trousers are also loose and shapeless, with the brown leather gaiters fastened over them. A grey woollen neck-cloth is worn.

Footwear: Stout brown leather boots are worn.

Accessories: The carrier is examining a sack with a label tied to the top.

248. Children's Nurse with Little Girl. 1908

Hair: The nurse's hair is swept up from a centre-parting to a chignon on the top of the head covered by the cap. The child's hair is cut in a fringe in front. The ends are turned under at the back.

Headdress: The nurse's small frilled muslin cap is perched up on the head and has streamers at the back.

Garments: The nurse wears a blue linen dress with a high collar and skirt just clearing the ground. The sleeves have some fullness over the elbows, with close-fitting lower sleeves attached. The white apron has frilled shoulder-pieces and a central frill above the narrow bib. The little girl wears a high-waisted white muslin dress with a pink sash.

Footwear: Only the tip of one of the nurse's black leather shoes is seen. The child wears white socks and white kid slippers.

Accessories: The nurse is holding a toy horse, attached to a ribbon.

249. Woman in Coat and Skirt. 1909

Hair: The hair is taken up over pads from a centre-parting into a chignon at mid-level at the back of the head.

Headdress: The hat of 'burnt' natural straw has a wide brim and is set back from the face, though perched over the chignon. It has a low crown and is trimmed with black satin ribbon.

Garments: The white cambric blouse has a high collar and a frilled decoration with small buttons, down the front, though it fastens at the back. The long coat of sand-coloured cloth is fitted to the waist and slightly flared in the skirt. It has revers and cuffs of black satin. The flared skirt, just showing the shoes, matches the coat.

Stockings: The black stockings are unseen.

Footwear: Black leather laced shoes are worn.

Accessories: The woman carries a small handbag of light-brown leather and an umbrella.

250. Landlady of Boarding-House or Lodgings. 1910

Hair: The hair is brought down a little over the brow from a centre-parting and then swept up over pads at the sides to a chignon a little below the crown of the head (unseen).

Garments: The dress is of printed cotton in green and white, with fairly full long sleeves and white collar and cuffs. Over it is worn a large black apron, covering the front of the bodice and most of the skirt.

Footwear: Only part of one black leather shoe is seen.

Accessories: The landlady is carrying a plate of food.